Yorkshire Dales

Northern & Eastern Area

Dalesman Publishing Company
The Water Mill, Broughton Hall,
Skipton, North Yorkshire BD23 3AG

First Edition 1999
Reprinted 2005

Text © Terry Marsh 1999
Maps by Jeremy Ashcroft
Cover photograph: Swaledale near Gunnerside
by David Tarn

A British Library Cataloguing-in-Publication
record is available for this book

ISBN 185568 132 3

Printed in China

Yorkshire Dales

Northern & Eastern Area

Terry Marsh

**Companion volume to
Yorkshire Dales Southern & Western**

Series editor Terry Marsh

Dalesman

The Yorkshire Dales: N & E

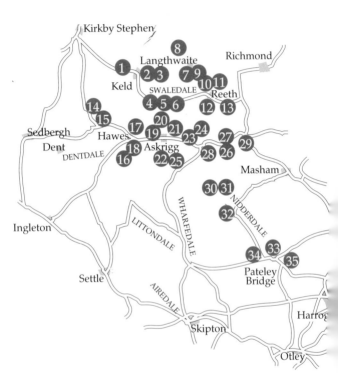

Contents

Nidderdale

INTRODUCTION

The Yorkshire Dales possess some of the most beautiful landscapes in Britain. They attract millions of visitors each year, for tourism and recreation, for study and for work. But there are already thousands of people here, 18,000 to be more precise, a viable community of residents who live and work within the boundaries of the national park. But while tourism is becoming increasingly important, the local economy is still dependent on farming.

This is a landscape of almost infinite variety, from wild mountain uplands to verdant riverside meadows, from vast expanses of limestone pavement to equally vast expanses of peat bog, from windswept summits to the hidden depths of subterranean passages. It is a landscape that attracts people from all backgrounds and for many differing reasons, whether it is simply to appreciate the scenery or to look more deeply into the history of the region, whether it is to pass by in a carefree way or to pause and study what lies beneath our feet and all around.

And the great range of possibilities is made all the easier by a penetrating network of roads and an even more extensive mantle of footpaths and bridleways, more than a thousand miles in total, that sits neatly on top of everything. Indeed, some of Britain's finest walking routes pass through the Dales: the Pennine Way cuts south to north; the Dales Way, from Ilkley through Wharfedale, across to Dentdale and into Lakeland; the Ribble Way begins life at Ribblehead and heads south to Settle before finally quitting Dales country, and the Northern Coast to Coast Walk flits happily across the northern part, for the most part taking an intimate look at delectable Swaledale.

Between this and the companion volume I have drawn together seventy walks, some circular, some linear, but all guiding you into a closer acquaintance with the Dales, for there is no better way to see the Dales than on foot. Walking in the Dales provides endless delight, whatever the time of year, whatever the weather.

This volume covers the North and East, exploring Swaledale, Wensleydale and Nidderdale; while Volume 2 takes you into the South and West, through Ribblesdale, Wharfedale, Airedale and Malhamdale, Dentdale and the Howgills.

It could be argued that Nidderdale is not part of the Yorkshire Dales National Park, which is true. But it is an Area of Outstanding Natural Beauty, and I prefer to think of its exclusion from the national park as a sad oversight on the part of some former bureaucrat, and an omission that should not be taken too seriously, so far as walking is concerned. And if it does not form part of the Yorkshire Dales National Park, it is unquestionably part of the Yorkshire Dales.

In the end, all that this tells us is that it is impossible to constrain by artificial boundaries a region that is more a sense of place than somewhere you can delineate on a map. The Dales don't cease to be the Dales simply because the area you are going into is managed by a different body of people.

Access by road

The Dales can be approached by road from all directions. From the north, from Kirkby Stephen, you can cut across into Birk Dale to Keld and upper Swaledale or strike south through the delectable Vale of Eden to Garsdale Head, Hawes and Wensleydale. From the south you head up from Skipton into Malhamdale, across to Settle and Ribblesdale or up to Grassington and Wharfedale. From the west, you enter Dales country at Sedbergh, turning a blind eye to the fact that you're in Cumbria as you head across to Garsdale or Dentdale. While from the east you come in from Richmond, Leyburn or Ripon.

Access by public transport

Sadly, the Yorkshire Dales are not as well served by public transport as they might be.

Rail: You can get around the fringes of the Dales easily enough, but there is little scope for getting right into them. The Leeds-Settle-Carlisle railway line provides one obvious and very attractive way, and, at Settle, this connects with services from the west.

For information specifically about trains ring 0113

224 8133 (Leeds), 01228 44711 (Carlisle), or 0345 484950 (national rail enquiries).

Bus: By bus there is a slightly better service, and most of the dales can be accessed this way. Some, however, have very limited services, often only once or twice a day and during summer months only. Bus services are changing all the time, however, so it is always wise to obtain up-to-date information from the appropriate tourist information centre (see below) before committing yourself to using public transport.

Some areas also have a postbus service — Wensleydale, for example — and this can be a useful, inexpensive and interesting way of getting about.

Accommodation

The Yorkshire Dales has a wide selection of accommodation — hotels, guest houses, B&Bs, self-catering and youth hostels. Expect many places to be fully booked during the main tourist seasons, but if you are prepared to go during autumn and the winter months, you will find numerous places that are inexpensive and welcoming.

Equipment

All walkers have their own preferences in the matter of equipment and clothing, but the following list may be found a useful reminder — rucksack (comfortable, well padded), boots, socks, trousers (or shorts, etc., but not shorts alone — at certain times of the year there are a lot of nettles), underclothes, shirt, midwear (e.g. pullover) and spare, wind- waterproof jacket and overtrousers, hat, gloves, maps, compass, torch (with spare battery and bulbs), whistle, first aid kit, survival bag or space blanket, food and drink, and (if necessary) insect repellent.

Do not be lulled into thinking that the proximity of villages from which help can be obtained means that you do not need to carry essential equipment. Even the shortest, simplest walks can become a severe test of patience and endurance if someone is injured and has to be left on the fells while help is brought.

Maps

The walks in this volume are covered on the following Ordnance Survey maps:

Outdoor Leisure Map 30 — Yorkshire Dales: Northern and Central areas

Explorer 26 — Nidderdale

Information

Yorkshire Dales National Park Information Service, Colvend, Hebden Road, Grassington, Skipton, North Yorkshire BD23 5LB (Tel. 01756 752748). You can also try their web site on: http://www.yorkshirenet.co.uk/visinfo/ydales

National Park Centres

Aysgarth Falls (01969 663424)

Clapham (015242 51419)

Grassington (01756 752774)

Hawes (01969 667450)

Malham (01729 830363)

Sedbergh (015396 20125

Yorkshire Tourist Board, 312 Tadcaster Road, York YO2 2HF (Tel. 01904 707961). You can also visit their web site on http://www.ytb.org.uk

Tourist Information Centres

Horton-in-Ribblesdale (01729 860333)

Ingleton (015242 41049)

Leyburn (01969 623069)

Pateley Bridge (01423 711147)

Reeth (01748 884059)

Richmond (01748 850252)

Settle (01729 825192)

Skipton (01756 792809)

SWALEDALE

The two great parallel dales of the Swale and the Ure provide by far the bulk of the walks in this volume. In many ways the Dales are similar — in the way they developed, the manner in which they were exploited by man for their mineral wealth (though Swaledale took the brunt of the industry), and in the growth of their towns and villages — but there is about Swaledale rather more of a feeling of insularity and self-containment.

You can drive right through Swaledale, of course, as you can with Wensleydale, but here, from the moment you enter the dale, whether from the west or the east, there is a greater sense of being shut in, of being closer to the pulse of the dale. Swaledale is not a main thoroughfare, Wensleydale is. The feeling of isolation and independence is further experienced as you explore Swaledale's only side valley, Arkengarthdale. Here you find small hamlets and numerous farming communities, and a great sense of being far away; exquisite for walkers, of course, but perhaps less so for those who earn a living here. Even so, the very remoteness brings its own beauty and, paradoxically, a companionship in solitude.

For many visitors, Swaledale is the most lovely of the Dales, with scenery and sensitive development which epitomise everything that is pleasing about the whole region. Its main attractions, however, are of the natural kind, from high heather moorland to splendid waterfalls, from bare hilltops to rich, green valleys bright in spring and early summer with wild flowers beyond number.

The dale, and the river that gives it its name, begins high on windswept moorland, far from civilisation — or so it seems. Then rough fell pastures appear, and a few windswept farmsteads before the river glides past the hamlet of Keld, its name of Norse derivation, and meaning 'a spring' or 'a place by the river'. Here the river goes one way and the road the other as they find their respective courses around Kisdon Hill.

Near Keld, the river begins to flex its muscles, putting on dashing shows at Wain Wath, Catrake and Kisdon Forces before effecting a more subdued entry into the main west-east thrust of the dale. There is great pleasure in these upper reaches, but equal if not greater enjoyment in starting to follow the river's course.

South of Kisdon Hill, and not quite on the Swale, is the village of Thwaite. The name itself means 'a clearing', another indicator of Norse and Viking influence, and this is also underscored by the use in Swaledale, and very few places else, of the name 'fell' for the hills, which elsewhere tend to be called simply 'moors'; there are exceptions to every rule, of course.

Thwaite was the birthplace of two brothers, Cherry and Richard Kearton, who were pioneers in the field of natural history photography. They were renowned naturalists and pioneered the use of hides to get close to their subjects. Not surprisingly, their interest in the natural world developed from their exploration as children of the gullies, fells and dales that surrounded them. They eventually moved away to London, but are said never to have lost their love for Swaledale.

Muker is the first sizeable village along the Swale, although it does set itself a distance from it. Its church was built in 1580 as a chapel of ease to Grinton, and has the distinction of being one of a very few churches built during the reign of Elizabeth I. With its consecration came an end to the hitherto weary traipsing across the fells of those whose mission in life it was to convey the dead for burial at Grinton. The 'Corpse Way' can still be traced down the length of the dale, and part of it is touched upon by walks in this book.

For walkers, Muker is a comforting place. There are shops here, a post office and tea rooms, and what a pleasure they can be when the light is beginning to fade and the cold air of evening breathes upon the valley.

At Muker the river changes direction, now heading roughly east and scarcely varying this course until way beyond Richmond. As the dale approaches Gunnerside, so the fells to the north are split by a great ravine; not so wide as that of the Swale to the north of Muker, but wide enough, and fashioned by rippling Gunnerside Beck. Up here, swathed in the flowing folds of the fells, men toiled long hours to win galena, or lead ore, from the hillsides. Their buildings and industrial machines, now in ruins, still litter the fellsides, but are a fine and important legacy for those with an interest in industrial archaeology.

From the dale bottom there is little to see of these mining scars, but even the slightest detour from the main thrust of the dale will bring you into contact with an old building here, a piece of rusted machinery there, and a score of places where the fellsides have been laid bare and lined with man-made gullies, or hushes, down which water, dammed higher up, was released to flush away surface soil to expose the prized minerals below.

The name Gunnerside is also of Norse derivation, and means 'Gunnar's pasture' or 'sett'. The village took the greatest force of the lead mining activity and so when this ended it was affected the most, standing for years with a look of despair and desolation. But that is no longer there, and the village now enjoys great popularity. It is a welcoming place; not even the greyness of its buildings is oppressing for they spread themselves across the fellside or in tight clusters, focused on the village shops and pub, the King's Head.

Between Gunnerside and Reeth there are a number of small hamlets — Low Row, Feetham, Blades and Healaugh, with its carpeted and florally dressed telephone box. There is a delightful way in which the cottages and houses have been built, dotted along the main roads or turning abruptly from them to create small oases of green. This almost haphazard development is typical of the dale and one of its endearing features.

In her book on Swaledale, Ella Pontefract says of Healaugh that it 'has a peaceful, but rather mournful air, as though it remembered former greatness, and harboured just a little discontent'. It was certainly famous in the past for hunting, in the days when wild boar and wolves roamed the dales, but whether today you would say it was mournful is another matter.

And so you arrive at Reeth, once the centre of considerable mining activity and the point at which Swaledale's principal tributary, Arkengarthdale, joins the valley.

The village, much larger than anything up-dale, with a wide range of shops, pubs, accommodation and information points, was established as a forest edge settlement, and holds a strategic position in the dale, so much so that it has acquired the title, capital of mid-Swaledale.

By the early 19th century, Reeth was a prosperous place, and found a good part of its wealth in an unlikely way, from knitting. Perhaps this is not as surprising or unlikely as I might suggest, since knitting was a key element in the local economy throughout the Dales. People knitted whenever they could, as a means of supplementing the family earnings, and produced anything from gloves to sailor caps. This trade, however, quickly died out when machinery replaced the traditional needles.

Today, Reeth is a renowned venue for local fairs, shows and festivals, and is an ideal place from which to explore the dale.

But this book does not finish with Swaledale once it reaches Reeth. Beyond lie more villages of varying size — Fremington, Grinton, Marrick and Marske.

At Marrick there is a 12th-century Benedictine priory, now an educational and residential centre. It was occupied by nuns from 1154 until the Dissolution of the Monasteries, after which it fell into ruin, with only a tower remaining. Later, however, it served as the parish church and a farm, and in the 1960s was converted into its present use.

Marske lies in a side valley, a peaceful and attractive retreat, with a 12th-century church dedicated to St Edmund and the imposing Marske Hall where the Huttons were the dominant family, producing two archbishops. In *The Yorkshire Pennines of the North-West*, W. Riley writes 'But don't you believe that the serpent never gets into Swawd'l. The dale has bred men of another kidney besides bishops.' He describes 'carryings-on' in the big houses, 'when the gentry wouldn't let their guests leave the table till they were too drunk to walk upstairs to bed'.

You can still become intoxicated in Swaledale, but it need not be as a result of drinking, except that form which involves drinking in the heady delights of the dale and its villages. And the beauty of this is that it involves no hangover, except the desire to return.

1 Ravenseat

At the top end of Swaledale lie two attractive, smaller dales that are little known to weekend walkers, Birk Dale and Whitsun Dale. The former takes the B-road over the moors to Nateby and Kirkby Stephen, while the latter, a seasonal alternative for the Northern Coast to Coast Walk, does much the same for walkers. This walk visits both dales.

Distance: 7½ miles/ 12km	**Type of walk:** *A mix of road walking and field paths*
Height gain: *655ft/200m*	
Walking time: *3-4 hours*	**Start/Finish:** *Keld. GR893011*

Keld youth hostel, a former shooting lodge, makes a good base for this walk for anyone spending more than a day in the area. It is surrounded by waterfalls and wild moorland, and is growing in popularity. Keld itself is the first village in Swaledale, and it has taken on the role of providing a welcome staging post for long distance walkers.

From the village set off up the B-road, following it for a little over a mile (2km) as far as High Bridge, where the road crosses the River Swale. Don't cross the bridge, but opt for a track heading upstream to a gate, and beyond that branch left between a wall on your right and a stream. Go through a gate to the right of a barn, and onto a riverside path. Follow this to a stone bridge, and cross at this point, continuing on the other side up to Firs.

Press on beyond Firs on a broad track, but when this turns left between walls, bear right alongside the on-going wall. Initially, the track climbs above the wall, but when it deteriorates to a path, you need to return towards the wall to cross a stile. Climb beyond to a cottage, and then take to its access track as far as a gate. Through the gate, leave the track, and keep left alongside a wall, before heading up to the unfenced B-road that runs through Birk Dale.

Turn right along the road and then take the surfaced lane running up to Ravenseat, a small, isolated farming community where you meet up with the route of the Coast to Coast Walk, which will now accompany you back to Keld.

Cross a bridge to enter Ravenseat and immediately go right across a narrow sleeper bridge spanning a small stream, to a gate. Go through the gate and shortly turn right again through a gated stile that brings you onto the eastern bank of Whitsundale Beck.

From here back to Keld the route is never in doubt as it heads through a landscape enhanced by a series of small waterfalls. Continue easily, passing through a number of gates, climbing half left to a barn, and then by a slightly higher level to the unexpected scenery of How Edge Scars and Over

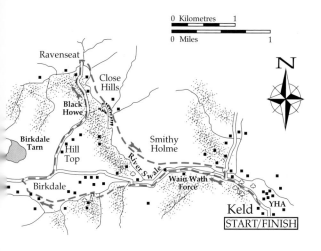

Mouth. Climb on a steeply ascending path, left, alongside a wall.

Above Oven Mouth, and after a gate in a fence, the path forks. Go right here to pass a dilapidated enclosure, Eddy Fold, and keep on until the farm of Smithy Holme is reached. A good path goes past the farm and soon drops to meet the Kirkby Stephen road at Low Bridge.

After a gate just before the final drop towards Low Bridge, look for a path going left above a collapsed wall. This leads above a limestone escarpment, Cotterby Scar, to meet the road climbing left to Tan Hill at a hairpin bend. At the road, turn right and descend to the valley road and so rejoin your outward route.

2 Kisdon Force

As waterfalls go, Kisdon Force, or Foss, is equalled by a number of other falls throughout Yorkshire. But it is the most dramatic of the falls along the River Swale, encased in surrounding fells, shrouded by riverside woodland and set in a deep gorge that was considered by Harry Speight, a 19th-century historian who devoted himself to the study of his native Yorkshire, to have 'the grandest combinations of rock and water scenery in the kingdom'. Many justifiably share this view.

Distance: 6½ miles/ 10.5km
Height gain: 805ft/245m
Walking time: 3-4 hours
Type of walk: On good paths throughout, but slippery when wet
Start/Finish: *Thwaite. GR892982. Limited parking*

The village of Thwaite today is a small cluster of cottages that ruggedly characterise the charm of this remote part of the Dales. But it is one of the earliest settlements in upper Swaledale, a Viking hamlet that was later the birthplace of Richard and Cherry Kearton.

Richard (1862-1928) and his brother Cherry (1871-1940) went to school in Muker (the school is now a tea room), and were later instrumental in developing the appeal of natural history. Richard photographed it, wrote about everything he saw, and lectured about it, while Cherry eventually became a very successful freelance wildlife photographer. They were among the first in this genre, and came up with the idea of using a portable hide to get close enough to birds to photograph them. In choosing a hide they were often quite inventive using, on a number of occasions, an artificial cow (which was frequently blown over), an artificial boulder, and tree trunks. To gain height, Cherry added saplings to his tripod legs, and stood on his brother's shoulders. At other times he swung across cliff faces on a rope, or hoisted ladders into trees. Before long they published 'British Birds' Nests', and soon followed this by 'With Nature and a Camera'. Their first lecture was given in 1897, the first of many that proved immensely popular. Richard produced sixteen books in total, while Cherry turned more to filming wildlife, especially African big game, a far cry from their quiet beginnings in Thwaite.

Turn right in front of the Kearton Guest House and shop, and a short way on leave the lane on a footpath (signposted for the Pennine Way), which you will be following as far as Kisdon. Stay with the on-going path, but ignore the signposted path to Angram. Keep on through a couple of squeeze stiles, then branch left with the Pennine Way across a field to a gate. Cross the next field, and in the following field, walk along the boundary and climb to the intake wall. After crossing the intake, branch right on a rising track through heather and bracken.

The path climbs for a while longer before levelling out, and continues past Kisdon House, at which you go through one gate and then left through another onto a walled lane. At the end of the lane, keep forward, still on the Pennine Way. The path roughly contours across the side of Kisdon Hill, high above the Swale, and gives splendid views before it eventually starts to descend to a footpath that branches right to Muker (used in Walk 3). Ignore this and keep forward.

A short way further on a path bears right to Kisdon Force. Go down this to view the waterfalls, and then return the same way. It is a narrow path through trees, and can be especially slippery after rain.

On rejoining the main Pennine Way path, follow it a short distance further, and when it bends sharply right to go down to cross the Swale, go with it. Having crossed the river, go forward on a rising path to cross above the diminutive, but attractive Keld Force, where the Pennine Way meets the Northern Coast to Coast Walk pioneered by the late Alfred Wainwright.

Now swap the Pennine Way for the Coast to Coast Walk by branching right onto a broad, rising, stony track.

Gradually the track levels out, and when it forks, branch right, steadily descending to meet the Swale again near the foot of Swinner Gill. Keep following the main track down the river, and just as the track starts to rise, as it approaches Rampsholme Bridge, branch right and cross the bridge.

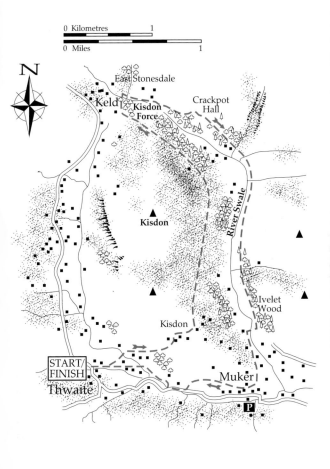

On the other side, turn right on a path beside a wall, to a gap stile. Through the stile, follow a paved pathway across meadows to reach Muker. These meadows in spring are especially beautiful and spread with wild flowers that are bright on the eye.

You reach Muker not far from the post office, from where the route continues, but if you need refreshments continue down to the main road, where there are excellent tea shops and a pub, as well as toilets. Then find your way back to the post office.

The walk continues by passing in front of the post office and going left past cottages to a gap stile at the entrance to a field. Go forward across a succession of fields, all accessed by gap stiles, until in the final field you can bear left towards farm buildings at Usha Gap. Here continue out to reach the road.

Turn right along the road back towards Thwaite. After 150yds/m, and just before a bridge, leave the road, on the right, through a gated gap stile beside a stream. The path now runs on beside a wall to another gap stile, beyond which you strike out across a field and then by an obvious field path and a trail of gated gap stiles back to the village of Thwaite.

3 Swinner Gill

Biting deep into the soft flanks of Gunnerside Moor, the craggy gap of Swinner Gill was once the scene of considerable lead mining activity. Now only ruins remain to tell of these former times, and only the sound of running water and the call of a passing bird fill the air where once the valleys echoed to the sound of men toiling long hours on and deep within the soaring hillsides.

Distance: *8½ miles/ 13.5km*
Height gain: *820ft/250m*
Walking time: *4 hours*

Type of walk: *A low and high level walk on good paths*
Start/Finish: *Muker car park. GR911978*

The beautiful village of Muker lies high up the dale, set amid much natural beauty. If you come away with the impression that little seems to have changed here, then that is probably because it's true. Old pictures of the village portray the cottages and houses, the church (originally dedicated in Elizabethan times) and the Victorian Literary Institute much as they are today, though the population has dwindled significantly from more than a thousand in the early part of the 19th century.

Leave the Muker car park and walk out to go left over the bridge towards the village centre, and then immediately branch right and go round the

27

Literary Institute. Go up the lane past the public hall, and then to the left of the post office and round the back of it, on a lane to Keld.

When, after the last cottages, the surfaced lane ends, keep forward on a rough, rising track, and as this bends left, leave it for an enclosed lane on the right, heading up the valley of the Swale.

A delightful track ensues, striking up the dale, a little above the valley bottom, and eventually, at a gate, reaches open pastureland, continuing then as a green track.

The path wanders on, never far from the River Swale, and then, at a gate, moves to run along the riverbank. As you move on up the dale, and approach the large left-hand bend of the river, look for a yellow waymark on a low wall, to the left, and head towards this, and then go forward across the next pasture to a gap stile (also waymarked). Head for an empty barn across the ensuing field on a broad grassy track; the way forward is clearly waymarked, and passes a number of derelict barns before reaching the remains of a walled lane, that leads you on through a gate, and guides you back down towards the Swale, as it approaches Kisdon Force.

The path presses on steadily and then rises to meet the Pennine Way at a track junction. Bear right, and keep on past the turning to Kisdon Force, and just as you approach the outskirts of Keld, branch sharp right, still on the Pennine Way, which has now met the Coast to Coast Walk, and go down to cross the Swale.

Over the Swale footbridge, bear left, and climb a short, steep embankment, turning right at the top and leaving the Pennine Way in favour of the Coast to Coast. Turn right over Keld Beck, and go through a metal gate, and then forward along a broad track, which now starts to climb above the Swale and Kisdon Gorge.

Keep following the broad track as it winds round, ascending almost all the time, and then, when it forks, branch left on a rising track to Crackpot Hall.

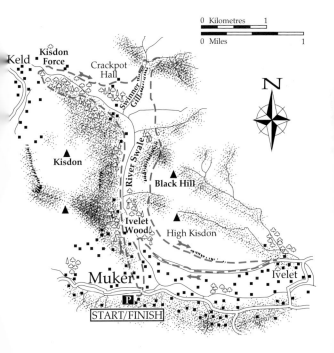

Lord Wharton built the hall for his gamekeeper, who looked after the herds of deer that patrolled these hillsides during the 17th and 18th centuries; the hall was still occupied well into the 20th century.

Keep to the left of the hall, and continue zigzagging on a rough track. Climb to another derelict building, and go on past this, bearing left to a gate, beyond which a high level path goes forward across the hillside to reach Swinner Gill.

High up in the gill, and accessible by a rough path, lies a concealed cave known as Swinner Gill Kirk. Here, during the years of religious persecution, Catholics came to hold their services in secret. Today the damp cave and its rocky ledges are home only to an abundant richness of wild flowers, ferns, mosses and liverworts.

Cross the bridge over Swinner Gill, and walk past a group of derelict mine buildings, and then immediately branch right to cross a tributary gill, and turn sharp right on a gently rising path.

Now an easy track leads on above Swinner Gill to a point directly above the Swale, reached at a ladder stile. Over this, keep forward on a grassy track through bracken and sedge, with excellent views both up and down the dale. The path drops to pass through a downfall of boulders and crosses a stream before continuing more or less horizontally, high above the valley.

Keep contouring across the hillside, eventually following a path beside a dilapidated wall. When the wall bears off to the right, high above Muker, branch left to a post on the continuing path across the hillside, heading in the direction of Ivelet.

For a while, the on-going route is not always obvious as it crosses grassy slopes, but in the distance near Kisdon Scar it can be seen traversing below the crags.

The on-going track continues to cross the hillside between Kisdon Scar, above, and Low Kisdon, then above Cock Crow Scar, which is directly above Calvert Houses. From there it descends gradually to meet the Gunnerside road. When you reach the road, turn sharply right, backtracking in the direction of Calvert Houses.

As you reach the first buildings at Calvert, take the track behind them. Eventually, just above Rampsholme Farm, the on-going road ceases to be surfaced, and here two tracks continue forward. Take the right-hand track, and when this forks a short way on, branch left on the more prominent track, and stay with this until you can leave it, doubling back to reach Rampsholme Bridge.

Over the bridge, turn right to a gap stile and then walk between a wall and the river to a gate on the left, and through the gate follow a paved way across fields back to Muker.

4 Gunnerside and Muker

This short walk linking three of upper Swaledale's delightful villages is simple and straightforward, and ideal for a short winter walk or when the weather is not too promising. It follows a surfaced route most of the way to the outskirts of Muker before returning via Ivelet on a low level route alongside the river.

Distance: 5½ miles/9km
Height gain: 425ft/130m
Walking time: 2½ hours
Type of walk: *Easy*
walking along roads and field paths
Start/Finish: *Gunnerside. GR951982*

Gunnerside is a grey stone village comfortably set among a complex landscape that is rich in history and industrial archaeology. The village dates from the time that the dale was settled by the Danes and the Vikings, and its name comes from Gunnar's saetr, meaning 'Gunnar's dwelling place'.

Leave the village on the road to the right of the post office, and follow the surfaced lane across the edge of moors, as it rises, and then gradually descends en route to Ivelet.

Where it meets Shore Gill, the road descends to cross it, rising on the other side to a junction. Here bear right, climbing for a while. Gradually the road levels off, before starting to descend towards Calvert Houses.

As you approach the first farm buildings at Calvert, take the track behind them. Eventually, above Rampsholme Farm, the on-going road ceases to be surfaced, and here two tracks continue forward. Take the right-hand track, and when this forks a short way on, branch left on the more prominent track, and stay with this until you can leave it by doubling back left to Rampsholme Bridge.

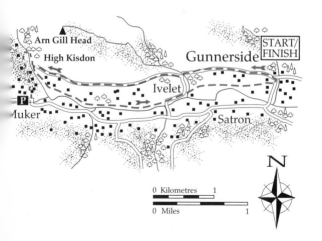

If you want to visit Muker, simply cross the bridge and follow a riverside path to a stile and then a paved pathway across fields to the village, where, along the main road, there are tea shops and a pub. Retrace your steps to Rampsholme Bridge.

Otherwise, go past the bridge and continue on a low-level footpath for Gunnerside. This leads to a gated gap stile beside a barn, beyond which a green track runs on across fields and through gap stiles to reach Ivelet Bridge, a fine single-arched bridge. It lies on an old corpse road from hamlets up the dale to Grinton Church, which until the consecration of the church at Muker in the 16th century was the only church with hallowed ground in Upper Swaledale.

Walk up into the village and at the telephone box turn right onto a minor road that soon leads to a gravel path with a cottage on the left and a barn on the right. At a waymark descend right on a narrow path to a footbridge spanning Shore Gill, with a fine view, characteristic of the dale, opening up ahead of rich green pastures, generously walled and barned. A series of meadows and stiles leads back to Gunnerside.

As your return path comes within sight of Gunnerside, ignore footpath signposts that send you down to the river bank. Branch left instead, for a gated gap stile and a green path that takes you across fields back towards Gunnerside, where you reach the village centre through a small estate of stone-built houses.

5 Gunnerside Gill and Melbecks Moor

In spite of the ruinous legacy of the mining industry that once flourished in the fells to the north of the Swale, and which is now encountered throughout this walk, the circuit, which climbs high across the bleak plateau of Melbecks Moor, is one of fascination for those interested in the industry of former times. In spring and early summer especially the moor is alive with grouse, young and old, and care is needed not to disturb the breeding birds.

Distance: *8 miles/13.5km*	*moorland walk; exposed*
Height gain: *1,280ft/*	*and bleak*
390m	**Start/Finish:** *Gunnerside.*
Walking time: *4 hours*	*GR951982*
Type of walk: *High-level*	

The gill, through which this walk begins, is a place seemingly set aside for lovers of industrial history. Above rise the sheltering fells, patterned by ancient walls, riven by man-made gullies and whitely etched after rain by cascading mountain streams.

From the parking space in Gunnerside, cross the nearby bridge and turn immediately left onto a footpath alongside Gunnerside Gill. This is soon deflected onto a brief walled pathway before opening into a rough pasture at a gate. Turn left.

When the on-going path forks, branch left following the 'Woodland Path' along Gunnerside Gill. The path climbs gently across lightly wooded slopes, then finally descends to rejoin the gill. Just as you leave the woodland, at a walled gap, go on a few strides and then right, through a gap stile, turning immediately left to walk beside the wall across two fields to a gated gap stile at which you rejoin the banks of the gill.

Keep on in the same direction, always following the course of the gill. Go past some old mine buildings and soon cross a step stile. Climb briefly to walk beside a wall, passing through the wall at a gap stile. Follow the on-going path as it rises gently. It continues steadily into the recesses of Gunnerside Gill, brief rises interspersed with longer stretches that are more level or rise only gently. The path eventually reaches a large complex of ruined buildings. Keep on beyond this, climbing to two cairns at a track/path junction at the base of an obvious broad rocky gully, one of the many man-made hushes created as part of the mining operations. Here, water that had been dammed higher up would be released to scour away the surface soil in order to expose the minerals beneath.

A path rises from the gill below and a track doubles back, climbing onto the hillside. Here turn right into the hush and follow its course upwards,

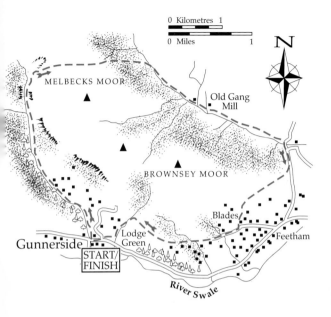

keeping an eye open for fossils, mainly crinoids and brachiopods, that are easy to spot in the surface debris.

At the top of the hush keep forward in the same direction for a short distance to intercept a broad track. Turn right onto this and follow it as it sweeps across the massive, gravelly top of Melbecks Moor. Eventually it descends to a bridge spanning Flincher Gill. Over the bridge turn right through a gate, and keep on above Mill Gill, also known as Old Gang Beck.

A short way further on, when the track branches,

keep right (horizontal) and go forward past a track junction, and always following the course of Mill Gill, now with the ruins of the Old Gang Lead Smelting Mill in view.

Keep on past the ruins — a fascinating place to explore — eventually to reach Surrender Bridge at a road. Turn right over the bridge, and follow the road for about 500yds/m. Then leave it, on the right, at a signposted footpath, a broad green swathe across the grouse moors of Feetham Pasture.

The path sweeps on across the moor and eventually leads to a gate at a wall junction. Beyond that, it continues as a rough-surfaced vehicle track leading down through the scattered farming hamlet of Blades to meet a road.

Turn right and follow the road until, now as a concrete track, it turns and descends left. Leave it here and keep forward on a broad grassy track above an intake wall. When the wall changes direction, keep forward, still on a green track. This keeps on across moorland, and at one point runs along the top of a low escarpment that offers a splendid view of the valley below.

Go through a nearby gate and keep on in the same direction. Eventually the track runs on to meet a wall near an isolated standing stone. At Barf End, not far from a stream which here produces an attractive waterfall, when the wall bends left, go with it, descending. When next the wall changes direction keep descending and about 80yds/m further on bear right to cross a stream.

Over the stream bear left to a wall, and then go down between stream and wall, recrossing the stream at one point and descending to meet a track. Turn right, cross the stream for a final time and then follow a descending green track towards Gunnerside. This soon joins a wall that guides you down to the edge of the village, a short way above the main road. Turn right along the road to return to the start.

6 Isles to Kearton

This short walk along the northern flank of Swaledale is full of interest, visiting Norse farmsteads, a medieval hunting lodge and an old corpse road before finishing along the banks of the river.

Distance: *4 miles/6.5km*	*incorporating woodland,*
Height gain: *575ft/175m*	*moorland and riverside*
Walking time: *2-2¹/₂*	*walking*
hours	**Start/Finish:** *Isles Bridge.*
Type of walk: *A*	*GR977975. Limited*
moderate walk	*parking.*

This interesting but brief walk begins from Isles Bridge, a crossing point of the River Swale, and a peaceful place to sit and watch the antics of oystercatchers, sand martins and dippers. Nearby is the small hamlet of Isles, more likely to be named, I suggest, after the appearance of pebbly islands in the flooded valley bottom in pre-Conquest days than from its association with a cottage named 'Belle Isle' after an island off the coast of Brittany captured by the British in 1761 during the Seven Years' War — there are, after all, numerous Belle Isles, not least the Isle of Man and Anglesey, and the Strait of Belle Isle in Canada. But who can say with certainty?

Begin by walking up to the main valley road and turn left for a short distance before branching right onto a track through trees. Once beyond the trees

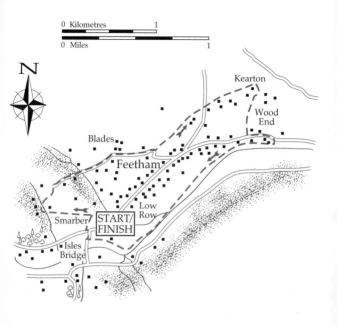

you follow a rising path across Friar's Intake to Smarber Farm.

The intake is said to be named after an 18th-century prospector named Fryer, who conjectured that there was lead in 'them there hills'; he was right, as remnant spoil heaps testify.

Smarber was one of the early Norse settlements, or 'saetrs', developed on the dale sides, above the generally impassable marshlands of the dale bottom. Later it became the site of one of Lord Wharton's hunting lodges.

Climb past Smarber, branching up to meet the lane running eastward to Blades.

This lane is part of the corpse road that, before the church at Muker was consecrated, ran from the top end of the dale to the consecrated land at Grinton, passing through Feetham, Kearton and Healaugh. It seems certain that, at the time, this would have been by far the easiest way up and down the dale. The lower parts, as well as being marshy, were often forested and inhabited by wild animals and robbers. Certainly, anyone carrying a corpse would want the least demanding route, and along its length, there would be slabs of stone on which the coffin could be rested. In reality, the 'coffin' would often be a wicker basket, to save weight on what, for anyone from the top end of the dale, would have been a two-day journey. If needed, an overnight halt was called not far from the route of this walk, at Riddings, where there used to be a barn known as the Dead House. Here the corpse would be left overnight, while the bearers would usually gravitate to the Punch Bowl Inn at Feetham for refreshments and accommodation.

Continue then, past Blades, as if heading for Feetham, on a route that is at least a thousand years old, and probably older. As the descending lane turns sharply right, leave it on the left to follow an enclosed track and then field paths across to meet the road to Surrender Bridge. Keep on across the road and go on as far as Kearton. Here turn right and go down to the valley road.

Turn left along the road for about 200m/yds until you can branch right into scrubby roadside woodland, Feetham Wood, and then down to the river bank. Turn right to follow a riverside path all the way back to Isles Bridge. On the way the path, which follows a low-level alternative of the Northern Coast to Coast Walk, runs for a short distance along the top of a wall, with a drop to pastureland on one side and the river on the other — a good sense of balance helps.

Over the stream bear left to a wall, and then go down between stream and wall, recrossing the stream at one point and descending to meet a track. Turn right, cross the stream for a final time and then follow a descending green track towards Gunnerside. This soon joins a wall that guides you down to the edge of the village, a short way above the main road. Turn right along the road to return to the start.

7 Flincher Gill and Great Pinseat

Superficially, there is a sadness about the barrenness that the old lead miners – 't'owd men', as they were known – have left on the moors north of Swaledale. But it is a sadness that serves to emphasise the beauty that is elsewhere all around, a beauty that is Nature in one of her forgiving moods, as she seeks steadily to repair the damage, or, in less despoiled parts, trains her flattering light on the rippling expanse of grouse-inhabited moorland. This walk begins by visiting the lead mines, before curving higher onto the moors that culminate in the rocky summit of Great Pinseat. A splendid moorland tramp concludes the walk.

Distance: *5 miles/8.5km*
Height gain: *755ft/230m*
Walking time: *3 hours*
Type of walk: *High moorland tracks with little*
shelter; not advised in poor visibility
Start/Finish: *Surrender Bridge. GR989999*

Surrender Bridge is named after the nearby Surrender Smelt Mill, and from it a broad track runs beside Mill Gill, or Old Gang Beck, as it is also known. 'Gang' in this context is not a group of workmen, but comes from the Old English word for a road. Old, or Auld, Gang suggests that these mines were probably already well established, if on a smaller scale, during Saxon times.

Head up the track and eventually pass Old Gang Lead Smelting Mill, built around 1770, and now undergoing some restoration, or at least preservation.

The remains here are particularly extensive and include furnace houses, flues and storage huts. This is certainly one of the more evocative of the remains of the lead mining era, and a careful exploration is well worthwhile.

Lead mining was no new activity, of course. The Romans mined lead, Cistercian monks held mining rights in their estates, and there is clear evidence that lead was mined during medieval times. The main period of activity, however, was from the late 18th century until the mid-19th. Most of the remains on these moors date from this time.

At Old Gang, the mix of ore and rock (called 'bouse') was gathered in large stone hoppers before reaching the dressing floor, where it was separated and cleaned. In order to extract the lead from the ore, smelting was necessary, and Old Gang was a smelt mill. The ore would be heated in a small hearth and its poisonous gases and impurities burned off. The residual metal was then channelled into moulds. The most efficient type of furnace, however, was the reverberatory furnace, which came into use in the 18th century, but needed a group of mines to keep it supplied.

One notable feature of many smelt mills was the flue. Large quantities of lead used to be lost when the fumes from the smelting process were exposed to air too early

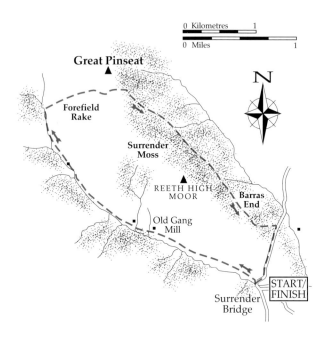

in the process. In the 18th century, it was discovered that if the fumes were directed into a long and horizontal chimney, lead would accumulate on its inner surfaces, and could be scraped off. The Old Gang has a steeply angled flue striking up the fellside above to a terminal stack.

For a time, the Old Gang site was leased by the London Lead Mining Company, the Quaker-run business, but they left the Swaledale area at the end of the 18th century.

Having passed the mill, ignore a branching track on the left, and keep forward to reach a gate near the bridge over Flincher Gill.

Beyond Flincher Gill lies Merry Field, where the mines were so rich that almost fifty per cent of what came out of the ground could be used; the other half, of course, was dumped – as you can see!

There used to be quite a community of workers and families here. The parish registers at Grinton show an entry for 1744, when Mary, the daughter of John Borras of Levell House, was christened; likewise William Bland, of Moor House, who was christened in 1806.

Traditionally, miners would travel a considerable distance to work here, lodging at the houses from Monday until Saturday, and bringing enough food with them to last all week.

At the gate, bear right, ignoring the bridge, and continue alongside Flincher Gill, moving steadily into an increasingly austere landscape. Keep following the on-going track as it climbs ever upwards along the course of Forefield Rake, a worked-out lead vein. Eventually, the track dips to cross a feeder stream, before rising to a track junction. Bear right at this point, heading now for the marginally higher ground of Great Pinseat.

The track continues across the bleak moorland, passing to the south of the trig pillar on Great Pinseat. The actual summit, which cannot be reached on a right of way, is just off the track, to your left, beside a drystone wall. In poor visibility, it is difficult to find, but at the best of times has only a limited view.

If you continue on the track – easy, windswept walking – you eventually meet the moorland road about 800yds/m north of Surrender Bridge.

8 Upper Arkengarthdale

The top end of Arkengarthdale is rarely visited by walkers. It was once a Norse settlement, and is traditionally a sheep farming area. This walk visits a number of remote farms, many of them dating from the 17th and 18th centuries. It can be bleak on these hillsides, but on a fine day, they are as beautiful as anywhere in the Dales.

Distance: 4½ miles/7km   *moorland walking on*
Height gain: 425ft/130m   *tracks and roads*
Walking time: 2-3 hours   **Start/Finish:** *Whaw*
Type of walk: *High*   *Bridge. GR982044*

Leave Whaw, heading roughly northward, until the road bends right, and here keep forward onto a track that leads below a plantation to Low Faggergill Farm. Just as you approach the farm, branch right on the track to High Faggergill, a lonely spot some distance up on the moors, which you will visit later.

Soon turn left through a gate to pass behind Low Faggergill and cross a couple of fields.

To your left the moors gather themselves into the depression of Great Punchard Gill, which in 1986, after hours of torrential rain, produced a tide of floodwater that roared down the gill into the main valley causing considerable damage. Flooding, particularly in this high and remote valley, is not something you hear much about, but the devastation in 1986, which came on the apron strings of Hurricane Charley, is not unusual. Harry Speight, the great Yorkshire historian, wrote in 'Romantic Richmondshire', in 1897, about flooding in the valley, explaining that the dale had been 'a complete wreck from end to end' on more than one occasion.

Cross walls and walk into the ensuing field, heading across more fields until you reach Hill Top Farm, and then carry on further to Dale Head Farm, crossing delightful moorland that in spring and early summer echoes to the call of the birds that find this an ideal habitat – curlew, redshank, snipe, lapwing and wheatear. Most of these birds are resident, but any wheatears you see have probably travelled all the way from Africa to be here.

Keep to the left of Dale Head Farm, following an access track that goes up and through Ravens Park Farm.

Now a change of direction begins the return leg, on a track that follows the intake wall. At Colt Park Corner, where the wall bends sharply, the onward route is not always obvious, but if you continue heading south-east you soon intercept a stream. Go left alongside a wall to a stile, and then cross a slab bridge. Now head uphill to High Faggergill Farm, aiming to the right of it.

Like many of the hillsides in the region, the moors here were once mined for lead. Above the farm is Faggergill

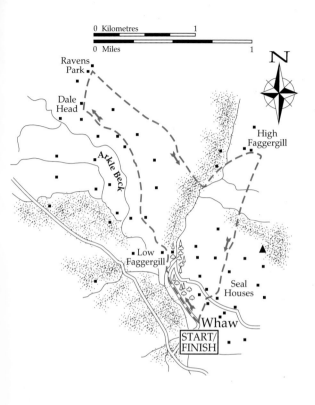

Mine, which produced lead into the early part of the 20th century.

From the farm, use its access to return to the valley. Lower down the access is surfaced and descends to a junction. Turn right for a little over 100yds/m, and then turn left over a stile and descend through four fields to return to Whaw.

9 Reeth Low Moor

The great expanse of Reeth Low Moor lies to the south of Langthwaite and Arkle Town in Arkengarthdale, and rises to the top of Calver Hill, a prominent landmark. The walk begins in Langthwaite, once an important centre of the lead mining industry, and visits nearby Arkle Town before striking up onto the moors and circling Calver Hill. As well as the familiar indications of old mine and quarry workings, the map here reveals a number of hut circles and enclosures that are of a much earlier time.

Distance: *6¼ miles/10km*
Height gain: *950ft/290m*
Walking time: *4 hours*
Type of walk: *Some high moorland walking,*
generally on good paths, but not suitable for poor visibility
Start/Finish:
Langthwaite. GR005024

From Langthwaite, an attractive village with a large church, dedicated to St Mary and built during the reign of George III, walk along the road to the nearby hamlet of Arkle Town as far as a path on the right (signposted: Fore Gill Gate) that sets off around diminutive Cumbers Hill. The onward route parallels Fore Gill, a steep-sided ravine with much evidence of mining. The right of way, however, stays above the gill, and isn't always easy to follow. Towards the top of the gill, turn sharply left to go through a gate in a wall and cross to a broad moorland track. Turn right and walk towards Fore Gill Gate, beyond which lies the moorland road linking Surrender Bridge and Langthwaite.

Without going through the gate, turn and walk away, heading south-east along the track used in Walk 10. This passes to the south of Cringley Hill and continues uneventfully across the wide moors to descend to the farm at Thirns, on the way joining the route of the Northern Coast to Coast Walk. As you progress, so the mound of Calver Hill becomes more distinctive and shapely.

There is a tremendous feeling of openness as you cross the moors. In spring and summer moorland flowers dot the landscape and the air is filled with the sound of birds. The height, of course, provides good viewing both up and down the dale.

From Thirns you climb to a higher cottage and about 400yds/m later turn left onto a moorland path that seems to be heading for Calver Hill itself. In fact, the path strikes almost due north, passing below the steep slopes of the hill, and becoming less distinct as you go. Calver Hill is a classic viewpoint, but, alas, there is no right of way to its summit.

Eventually you cross the Arkengarthdale road and can follow the access track to West Raw Croft Farm from where a walled lane runs down to a footbridge spanning Arkle Beck. Across the beck, turn left and follow a beckside path that soon brings you onto a walled lane. Go forward, passing a footbridge, and follow the on-going track back to Langthwaite, reaching the village near the Red Lion pub.

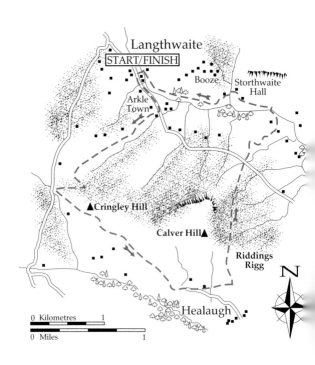

10 Arkle Town and Fremington Edge

This moderately easy walk, ideal for good winter conditions, makes an exaggerated loop around the attractive pasturelands of Arkengarthdale, beginning along a stretch of the Northern Coast to Coast Walk as it crosses Reeth Low Moor. Half way round the walk condescends to visit the neat cluster of grey houses at Arkle Town, and Langthwaite, too, if you've a mind, before climbing onto the long moorland top of Fremington Edge.

Distance: *12½ miles/ 20km*	**Type of walk:** *A fairly demanding high moorland walk*
Height gain: *1,510ft/ 460m*	
Walking time: *5-6 hours*	**Start/Finish:** *Reeth. GR038993*

Once the centre of extensive mining activity, Reeth stands perched on a green plateau near the confluence of the River Swale and Arkle Beck; indeed the Old English meaning of the village's name is 'at the stream'.

Reeth holds a strategic position at the edge of a former forest, and its shops, inns and cottages gaze out across the luxurious vale it commands. In recent times, it has acquired the title of capital of mid-Swaledale, and it certainly stands in a splendid situation. In fact, as Ella Pontefract and Marie Hartley pointed out in 'Swaledale' you can imagine that long ago Reeth 'came exploring up the dale, and found this flat piece of land which fitted it, and stayed there. It seems to smile, as though pleased with life.'

Leave Reeth on the road for Gunnerside until, a short way out of the village, you can turn right onto Skelgate Lane, a walled lane rising onto the moors above. Follow the lane to the intake wall and go through a gate. Keep on with a wall on your left-hand side, and when it bends to the left, keep ahead on a prominent path past a large cairn, now with Calver Hill in view ahead.

The on-going track sweeps splendidly across the moorland slopes, never far from the intake wall, and at times running beside it. Shortly after a footpath sign, the on-going track branches. Go left, and head down towards Thirns Farm.

Pass Thirns and go forward alongside a wall, and shortly, as the track forks again, near a bend in the wall, branch right, rising onto the moors. High on the moors below Calver Hill, when the track forks yet again, branch right once more and follow a track parallel with a wall.

The on-going track continues across the moors beyond Calver Hill and below the heather-covered Cringley Hill, and leads clearly to meet the road from Surrender Bridge. Just as it approaches the road at Fore Gill Gate, however, turn sharp right to

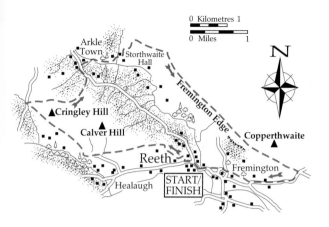

return in an easterly direction around the northern slope of Cringley Hill. The track sweeps on in a generous arc across the moor above Arkle Town, and eventually comes down to join the Arkengarthdale road. When you reach it, turn left and go down into Arkle Town, and just after having crossed Fore Gill Beck, turn right. At the bottom of the lane, just before the last row of cottages, go through a gated gap stile on the right.

Follow a path through an old graveyard possessing a number of 18th-century gravestones. At the bottom, go through another wall gap onto a descending path high above Arkle Beck to reach a footbridge. Over the bridge, turn right on a broad track, passing a barn, and, a short distance on when this forks, rise left, on a track that leads to a junction at a blue metal gate.

Through the gate, turn right and go down to a

footbridge and ford near Storthwaite Hall Farm. From the footbridge, go in front of the farm, and then immediately left on a rising, walled lane that takes you up to a large, open pasture. Keep forward along the left-hand edge of the pasture, to a gate in the top intake wall. Through the top gate, turn right on a bridleway (signposted to Hurst) that climbs up a gully, just off to the right, towards a conspicuous cairn on a nearby hillock.

The rising track zigzags through quarry workings to reach Fell End, and is waymarked. It eventually clambers onto the large moorland expanse of Fremington Edge, still passing through an area of mining dereliction and spoil. From a prominent cairn (not the one seen from the valley below), a broad grassy track cuts across the moorland towards a distant wall, and then runs along Fremington Edge.

When you reach a wall junction, turn right through an old gateway, and then keep forward with the wall on your right-hand side, heading up onto Fremington Edge Top. When you meet a fence and wall junction, near a gate on the right, keep forward, continuing in the same direction, alongside the ridge wall.

Eventually the on-going track moves away from the wall a little, and goes down to a road. Turn right, and descend for about three quarters of a mile (1.5km), taking care as you do so – there are two steepish descents and long stretches where there are blind bends and no verge. Just past the entrance to West Hagg, leave the road, on the right, through a gated gap stile, at a footpath signposted to Fremington.

Go across the ensuing field to a gap stile in the far left corner, and then keep on in the same direction, always following the course of a wall, but on one occasion changing sides of it, until you reach the outskirts of Fremington. After an open field, near a farm, switch back across the wall, in due course going on to meet a rough, walled lane. This joins a surfaced lane in High Fremington. Turn left and follow the lane through the village, and then just after The Brambles, leave the road, on the right, at a signposted footpath through a gate. A short way further on, when the track forks, branch left, and go down to a gate at a wall junction. Beyond the gate, go forward for about 40yds/m, and then go through the wall on the left at another gated gap stile.

Cross the ensuing field to a stile beside a gate, beyond which you cut across a field corner to reach the main road at Reeth Bridge. Cross the bridge to return to the village.

11 Arkengarthdale

This easy walk is a delightful introduction to Arkengarthdale, and one that certainly encourages you to explore further up the dale, or across the high moors that rise above it. Diminutive Arkle Town is the turning point for this outing, which simply heads up one side of the valley and down the other, before finally returning to Reeth via the neighbouring hamlet of High Fremington.

Distance: 6¹/₂miles/ 10.5km
Height gain: 330ft/100m
Walking time: 3 hours
Type of walk: Easy

walking through countless pastures
Start/Finish: Reeth. GR038993

As well as having a foot firmly planted in Swaledale, Reeth, where this walk begins, also belongs to Arkengarthdale, the only large tributary of the Swale. And where Swaledale is a rather narrow dale, Arkengarthdale by comparison has a feeling of openness and freedom, though it lacks the expansive beauty of Swaledale. Even so, the road up beside the Buck Hotel beckons like an impatient child, urging you to see what the hidden dale beyond has to offer.

The dale is named after Arkil, the son of Gospatrick, who held the estate before the Norman Conquest, and that alone tells of the dale's ancestry. Further up the dale, strange names also tell of former times: 'Whaw', for

*example, means 'an enclosure for cows', while 'Booze',
attractive as it might be to suppose it is a place where
alcohol flows freely, actually means nothing more than a
'house by the bend (or bow) in the river'. Booze, alas, is
completely boozeless.*

Walk up the Arkengarthdale road until, just after a
left bend, you can leave it, on the right, near the
entrance to Sleights Brow. Here, go through a gated
gap stile onto a footpath (signposted to
Langthwaite). In the ensuing field go slightly left to
a gap stile, the first of a long series of stiles as the
on-going path traverses numerous walled pastures.

The way forward is always obvious and
waymarked, and it gradually brings you to a large
sloping pasture where Arkle Beck comes into view
for the first time. The route now continues as a
broad grassy track. Do not be tempted into
following a vehicle track across a bridge near the
farming hamlet of Castle. Instead, leave the track
and keep on crossing fields by a continuing line of
gap stiles.

Eventually, the path reaches a metal gate at a wall
corner and then continues as a broad grassy track
as it passes East Raw Croft Farm, heading for the
neighbouring West Raw Croft. Ignore the turning
to East Raw Croft and go forward to cross a stream
and a gap stile, and then on towards West Raw
Croft. Go through a gate near the farm, and then
continue ahead on a broad vehicle track across a
sloping pasture.

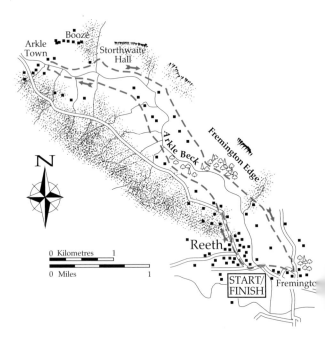

Keep forward to a red metal gate at a wall corner, and go forward through this on a continuing track beside a wall. This guides you to the top edge of a wooded slope above Arkle Beck, and a wooden gate. Through the gate bear left, away from the wall, rising across an undulating rough pasture to a fingerpost. From it, continue on a grassy path across fields, using gap stiles.

At a wooden step stile, the path finally descends to run close by Arkle Beck, flanked by lichen-covered alder, and soon passing through a gated gap stile to walk alongside the beck. A short way on you reach a footbridge spanning the beck, but before you can cross it you need to tackle in-flowing Fore Gill Beck, which in spate can be awkward.

Over the footbridge, begin the return leg by turning right on a broad track past a barn, and when the track forks, branch left on a rising bridleway. The track leads to a junction at a blue metal gate. Here, turn right on a bridleway (signposted to Fremington) that will take you most of the way back to Reeth. The bridleway circles round to a footbridge and ford, near Storthwaite Hall Farm.

Go up to pass in front of the farmhouse, and then bear right on a walled track that continues down to enter a large open pasture. Cross the pasture, going slightly left through a wall gap, beyond which an on-going broad green track returns to the bank of Arkle Beck, and soon passes a footbridge.

Go past the footbridge to a gate and then branch left at a fork to go up to Heggs House Farm. The bridleway passes behind the farm, rising to a gate. Through the gate go left, and soon turn right to resume the original direction.

The on-going path follows the line of a dilapidated wall and fence for some distance, and keeps on to pass Castle Farm. Ignore a ladder stile on the right, and keep on above the intake wall, which gradually descends to the right; the path simply follows the wall, descending eventually to a gate. Beyond the gate, the path continues downward through light woodland and finally arrives at a point just above Arkle Beck. Immediately, however, it branches left, away from it, on a rising track. Keep following the prominent on-going track that curves round, always beside a wall.

Further on, as a grassy path, the route continues to a gate at the end of a walled green lane. Go along this, with fine views across the valley to Reeth, perched on its hill end. When the green lane meets a surfaced lane, turn right and go down to High Fremington.

Go through the hamlet until, just after a cottage (The Brambles), you can leave the lane, on the right, along a path through a gate. Keep forward, and then branch left at a fork, now heading for Reeth Bridge. After a gated gap stile at a wall junction, go on for about 80yds/m to pass through a wall at a gap, and then bear right across the ensuing field.

The path ends by cutting briefly across a field corner to reach the main road. Turn right over Reeth Bridge to return to the village centre.

12 High Harker Hill

There is a tendency to think that most of the lead mining that went on in Swaledale was confined to the northern moors, but, as this walk demonstrates, there was a good deal of it to the south of the valley, too. From earlier times is Maiden Castle, perched high on a shoulder of High Harker Hill and reached by a minor diversion. It is certainly prehistoric, and may be as early as Bronze Age.

Distance: *7 miles/11km*
Height gain: *985ft/300m*
Walking time: *3-4 hours*
Type of walk: *High*

moorland walk on good tracks; little shelter
Start/Finish: *Reeth.*
GR038993

Leave Reeth on the Gunnerside road, but just after the fire station turn left into Langhorne Drive. At the bottom of the drive, turn right and continue past the doctor's surgery beyond which the road surfacing ends and the lane presses on as a walled track. When this bends (signposted to Harkerside: Grinton) follow it down to a gate, and a few strides further on cross a narrow footbridge.

Bear right and cross two fields to reach the Swale bridge. Over the bridge, go forward to a fence corner about 150yds/m distant, and there turn right through a gate to walk alongside a fence to a field corner. Cross a stile and bear half-right in the next field on a bridleway that heads back to the River Swale. Now walk alongside the river until, after a stile, you can climb half-left away from the river to follow the on-going bridleway, now beside a wall. This leads you on towards a road, finally reached a few strides beyond a gate.

At the lane, turn left for 400yds/m until, directly above Stubbin Farm, you can leave the lane, turning sharp right onto a rising vehicle track that cuts south-west onto the moor, through bracken and heather dotted with juniper.

If you want to visit Maiden Castle then, instead of turning sharp right onto the vehicle track, turn rather more to the south-east, climbing onto the moor. Maiden Castle is barely 200yds/m away, and from it, you can strike south-west across trackless ground to rejoin the rising vehicle track.

Maiden Castle, given its position and layout, is thought to be an early British camp, originally built as a defensive retreat. Later, lying as it does not so far from the Roman Fort at Bainbridge, it is likely that the site was occupied during Roman times, if only as an overnight halt.

The on-going track, used by estate managers, does not always correspond with the routes shown on the map. The track, however, winds up to the spoil heaps of Harker Lead Mine, and finally reaches a junction about 200yds/m distant from an isolated building. Here turn left and continue climbing onto the vast top of High Harker Hill, where a

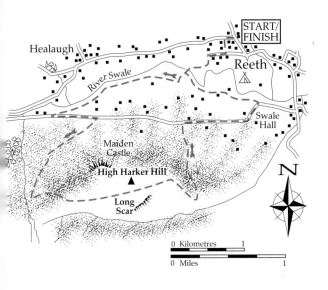

bridleway signpost is encountered.

Keep following the vehicle track across the top of the hill and on to Harkerside Moor, where it finally begins to descend through prominent earthworks.

The earthworks are thought to have been constructed by the Brigantes, an early English tribe conquered by the Romans during the reign of Antoninus Pius (AD138-161). The Brigantes occupied the region south of the Antonine Wall, extending to the Humber estuary in the east and to the River Mersey in the west. It is probable that the earthworks on Harkerside Moor were part of an actual or intended hill fortification.

Keep on down to a track junction near a small stream culvert, and here turn left heading roughly north on another vehicle track.

The track guides you down off the moor to meet a surfaced road directly opposite Bleak House. Turn right and follow the road towards Grinton. Keep following the lane for about half a mile until, just after a steep descent, you can leave it, on the left at a bend, for a signposted bridleway through a metal gate set back a few strides.

Having passed through the gate, the on-going path steers you down to meet and walk beside the Swale for a while before branching away as a walled lane that shortcuts a loop in the river. At a gate, the path breaks free of the walled lane, but keeps on in the same direction alongside an on-going wall.

Eventually, the path comes back to rejoin the Swale, and when it does bear right to follow the river bank back to Swale bridge. Cross the bridge and turn right, and cross two fields to a narrow footbridge at the foot of a walled lane. From here, retrace your steps back to Reeth.

13 Marske and Marrick

Marske, built along Marske Beck, is different from the usual type of Dales village in having a number of large houses rather than the customary, smaller cottages. There are a number of walking possibilities from Marske: this walk heads for nearby Marrick, renowned for its 12th-century Benedictine priory, the remains of which have now been converted to educational uses.

Distance: *5½ miles/9km*
Height gain: 655ft/ 200m
Walking time: *3 hours*

Type of walk: *Easy, pastoral walking*
Start/Finish: *Marske. GR104004*

From the village centre walk down Cat Bank, the minor road leading to Downholme Bridge. Go past Marske Hall, and then climb along the road until at its highest point on a bend you can leave it, on the left, at a signposted footpath for Downholme Bridge.

Leave the road at a gap stile, and in the ensuing field go half right, descending across the field slope, to a hedge gap. In the following large open pasture, go half left towards a stand of trees, and then keep forward to a field corner ahead, not far from which there is a gap stile. Go through the gap stile, and forward along a field edge above the River Swale following a fenceline downfield to a gate. And in the next field keep on in the same direction, never far from the river until you meet the road near Downholme Bridge.

You meet the road immediately adjoining the bridge at a signposted gap stile. Then turn right, up the road, for about 400yds/m, until the River Swale starts to bend away and there leave the road, on the left, through a metal gate, onto a broad track. Keep forward through a gate and continue along the edge of woodland, and crossing Oxque Gill.

Press on to reach Low Oxque Farm, and having past it, keep forward to a gate, continuing along a broad farm track. Keep following the track, always forward, beyond Marrick Park Farm, and then start to rise gently, passing a couple of lime kilns. Continue ascending to go past the Old Vicarage Farm. Keep going along the broad track until, on the outskirts of Marrick, you reach an isolated building, Park Lodge, and here bear right onto a rising track that runs into a brief walled section from which the escape is through a gap stile.

The path skirts dilapidated sheds, gently climbing until, at its highest point, the fields open out and a more satisfying prospect of rolling pastures reveals itself. Now gently descend to a broad track serving Nun Cote Nook Farm.

At the track go right, through a gate, and almost immediately left, continuing across broad pastures to the cottage at Ellers. Pass around Ellers and cross Ellers Beck, then slant up the next two fields to a gate near the access to Hollins Farm.

Follow the access track right for a short distance, and then, without entering Hollins farmyard, go left, passing a small copse to a stile. Cross the next field to a wall, and follow the wall left and, just as it enters a confined pathway, use a gate on the right to cross the ensuing field diagonally to gain a road, once an important link between Reeth and Richmond. Turn right down the road to return to Marske.

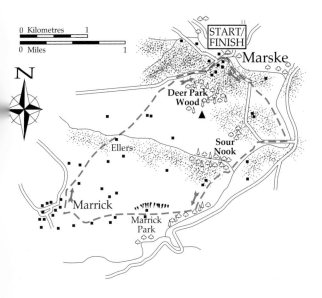

WENSLEYDALE

Of all the principal Dales, Wensleydale is alone in not being named after its river, the Ure, at least not since the 18th century when joint use of Wensleydale and Yoredale (or Uredale) ceased. The name Yoredale has, however, travelled through history because it was given as a name to a variety of rock first studied here by geologist John Phillips (1800-1874), who was also keeper of the York Museum from 1825 until 1840.

The Ure rises high on Lunds Fell, not far from today's border with Cumbria (previously Westmorland), and so by definition this must be the starting point of Wensleydale, though by common consensus the dale begins where the Ure turns the corner, not far from the Moorcock Inn.

Ure Head, the source of the Ure, lies at 2,132ft (650m) above sea level on a windswept plateau that looks out across the dale below to the colossal and amorphous mass of Baugh Fell and the rather more shapely summits of Wild Boar Fell and Swarth Fell. Here, in spite of the remoteness and harsh terrain, is a quiet vibrancy, a rich greenness that will follow the river throughout its course. Beyond the watershed – which, incidentally, is also the British watershed – in Cumbria lies the Vale of Eden, and some of this tranquil and naturally beautiful 'Edenness' spills over into upper 'Uredale'.

The valley bottom has long been cultivated, and

farms dot its length as they have done since the land was first inhabited. But the moors are never far away, rising above the intake walls, brooding over the scene. The line between the two is today marked by an ancient thoroughfare known as the High Way. This was a route used for trade, travel and brigandage, as well as by that remarkable noblewoman Lady Anne Clifford, who owned extensive lands and property in the region, and was a frequent traveller between them.

At the Moorcock junction, the dale is joined by the road through Garsdale which provides a good link with the west of the country, reaching out, as it does, to Sedbergh and the M6 motorway beyond. By the time the river reaches the Moorcock, it has lost half of its height, and here flows at only 985ft (300m).

Because these upper reaches of the valley are so beautiful, the walks that follow begin with one that extends to the very border of the county, at Hell Gill, before returning along the famous High Way. And this, more so than downriver, is very much walking country; you can drive through it, of course, but there are fewer honeypots at which to park the car for the obligatory trek to a nearby waterfall or ruined castle. Instead, you have to get out and explore rather further on foot.

For the most part the river ploughs an easy, peaceful furrow through the dale. But it is fed along the way by numerous becks draining from the flanking hillsides, which change the river's quiet chatter to the voice of a raging torrent that floods fields and properties along its length.

And those hills, without which there would be no dale, unlike Swaledale to the north, do not lean on the valley. Here they are far more laid back, and take a slightly more relaxed and distant view of things. As a result, the whole landscape of the dale is quite different from others, with the hills seeming to end in a uniform series of ledges formed where the softer layers of rocks have been worn away. They are a common feature of Wensleydale, a unique characteristic that forms an ever-changing background to the developments in the valley below.

Different, too, is the number of side dales that join the main thrust of the valley – Cotterdale, Raydale, Bishopdale, Walden and Coverdale – like branches on a tree. Some, as Ella Pontefract describes in *Wensleydale*, are 'miniatures of ... graciousness and repose; some have a fierce, untamed beauty; some rest quiet and secure in their own loveliness; some are shut away like secret, forgotten valleys.' And as you venture into these off-shoots it becomes possible to glean some feeling of how Wensleydale itself may have been hundreds of years ago, for there is about all of them a timelessness and individuality that is special and unique.

Yet in spite of all these unique qualities and air of foreverness, Wensleydale is no different from the other dales in the way it has grown under the influence of man.

The dale has probably been inhabited since the New Stone Age (about 3000 BC), when grain was cultivated and a primitive agriculture developed that was based on farming and hunting. From Bronze Age or earlier times a small henge survives at Castle Dykes south-west of Aysgarth, there is a large circle of stones at Carperby, and there are the remains of hut circles not far from Wensley. The remains of a village have been found at Semerwater in Raydale.

The Brigantes moved into the region about 300 BC, and brought with them a broader culture of farming, metalwork and pottery. Later came the Romans, though little evidence of their occupation of the Dales remains; neither the land nor the British climate was to their liking. Even so, their presence is particularly well noted above Bainbridge, where they had a fort, on Brough Hill, which was occupied from about AD 80 until they left Britain altogether. From Bainbridge one of their roads crosses the slopes of Wether Fell to Ribblesdale and on through Chapel-le-Dale to Ingleton.

After that, the development of Wensleydale differs little from the other dales. The Norsemen came and settled the area, and left behind many place names to tell of their presence. Later came the Normans who built the great abbeys, churches and castles, and it is the handiwork of the monks following the Norman Conquest which did much to fashion the dale into the form that largely remains today. The monks, like their predecessors, farmed the dales, constructed mills along the fast-flowing watercourses, and developed industries that continued to flourish long after the monasteries themselves were dissolved in the 16th century.

But not all the land was used, or usable, for farming. A good part of the landscape was 'waste', and suitable only as hunting forest, which was just what the Norman lords wanted. But gradually the cleared areas expanded until by the 17th century clearing activity was at its height. Then it was that many of the farms and manors were rebuilt, and began to gather into nucleated villages both for protection and common enterprise. The farms grew, for farming was still the main occupation, and the dale became richer as new industries began and existing ones were expanded so that the result was a busy and extended self-supporting community with its own identity – Wensleydale.

Hawes has long been a focal point of upper Wensleydale, though its origins are not as ancient as the haphazard, seemingly unplanned arrangement of its streets and buildings, leads you to suppose. There was little here when many of the villages tucked away in the folds of surroundings hills, now quiet retreats, were a-bustle with their own markets and fairs. Ella Pontefract observed that Hawes has 'no particular beauty, only the charm of a place admirably suited for its purpose'.

The town lies cradled among the hills, on the south bank of the still young River Ure as it meanders across the alluvial flats of Wensleydale. To the north lie the squat puddings of Great Shunner Fell and Lovely Seat, while to the south, on either side of the broad and beautiful Sleddale, rise the moorland summits of Dodd Fell Hill and Drumaldrace, the latter known locally as Wether Fell.

Not far from Hawes is a smaller village, Gayle, and the two almost blend together. But they do show some contrasting characteristics. Hawes by comparison is new and developing, Gayle is rather older and not progressing much at all. The village lies at the foot of Sleddale, beneath the great mound of Dodd Fell Hill, and its fame today rests largely on the fact that the Pennine Way marches through it before tumbling into Hawes.

To the north lie Hardraw and Sedbusk, the latter perched on the side of rising ground and seeming to deliberately want to distance itself from everything that's going on down below. Hardraw, by comparison, can hardly avoid the attention because here you will find Hardraw Force, a quite stunning spectacle, especially after prolonged rain; it is unquestionably one of Yorkshire's most impressive waterfalls. Twice, in the winters of 1739 and 1881, the weather here has been so cold that the waterfall froze solid. At other times, there has been so much water that the amphitheatre into which the fall cascades and the nearby pub and cottages were seriously flooded. And 'amphitheatre' is not an inappropriate word, because it was found to have such good acoustic qualities that in about 1885 the people of Hawes organised brass band concerts here, a tradition that has recently been revived.

And so you can go on down the length of the dale, with tales of waterfalls and attractive villages, of quiet corners and stunning views, of local characters and folklore, and scenery that has graced many a calendar, and still does. There is simply so much in Wensleydale – Bainbridge, Askrigg, Worton, Aysgarth – where there are yet more popular falls – Carperby, Redmire, West Witton, Middleham, Wensley and Leyburn. Each of these places has its own characteristics, its own tale to tell, and each plays an important part in the greater picture that is Wensleydale. The walks that follow endeavour to lure you into some of these places to experience the vibrant luxury of Wensleydale for yourself.

14 Hell Gill and the High Way

This long, steady walk is simply splendid and takes you almost to the source of the River Ure, which flows through Wensleydale. The turning point is Hell Gill, the boundary with adjoining Cumbria, from where we trace the route back towards Hawes followed by the redoubtable Lady Anne Clifford as she travelled this countryside in the 17th century. The scenery is outstanding, and the walk best kept for a long summer day, though it is not difficult and could be undertaken at any time of year.

Distance: *13¹/₂ miles/ 21.5km*	*fairly demanding; good paths*
Height gain: *985ft/300m*	**Start/Finish:** *Appersett.*
Walking time: *6 hours*	*GR858907*
Type of walk: *Long and*	

Appersett is a small, attractive village at the upper end of Wensleydale, but invariably passed through by visitors bound for the delights of nearby Hawes; that's a pity, because Appersett, with its village green and cluster of old cottages, has its own place in the scheme of things, and was originally a Norse settlement.

Walk out from Appersett on the Sedbergh road and cross the bridge spanning Widdale Beck. A short way on leave the road over a ladder stile on the left, and go right, alongside a wall, until you approach New Bridge, which crosses the River Ure. As you reach the bridge, don't cross it, but go left over a stile and walk alongside the river, on its true right bank. The onward route is now marked by stiles and gates, and crosses a succession of riverside, or near riverside, pastures.

Keep on to pass to the left of Birkrigg Farm, and cross more pastures. Nearby Hollin Bank is especially pleasing in spring and early summer when it is bright with wild flowers. Here the route takes you away from the river for a while, but gradually you come back to rejoin it. Off to your left is the course of the old Wensleydale railway that once travelled up and down the valley to Garsdale and beyond; what a tourist attraction that would be if it were ever reopened.

Gradually you approach Mossdale Head Farm. Pass in front of the farm and go forward to a bridge spanning Mossdale Gill. Cross the bridge and climb on the other side beside a wall and turn through a gap. Now cross the corner of a field and go down to reach the A684 at Thwaite Bridge. Cross the road with care, and go forward to cross the river, then go left through gates on a track signposted to Yore House.

The path now strikes across numerous fields, below the small plantation of Cotter and on to Yore House. Beyond, turning towards the Vale of Eden, you head across more pastures to Blades

Farm, where refreshments are usually available.

Continue by going round the back of the buildings at Blades, through a couple of gates, and then on towards a footbridge. From the footbridge, turn sharp right and soon go left alongside a woodland strip. Keep on through two more gates and cross Cowshaw Hill, a low drumlin, and a relic from the last Ice Age. Press on to reach Beck Side Farm, and then traverse more pastures just above the Ure to reach Low West End Farm.

Go past Low West End on its access track, heading initially for How Beck Bridge, but then cutting away on a rising track that continues the route northward to Green Bridge. Here you cross the infant River Ure, which rises only a short distance to the east, on Lunds Fell. A short distance further you reach Hell Gill Bridge, the turning point.

Hell Gill Bridge is a fine single arch of stone and dates from 1825, replacing an earlier structure, and a small stone in one of its parapets is thought to be an old boundary stone between Yorkshire and what was then Westmorland. William Camden, writing in the 16th century, mistakenly took the gill for the Ure, his perception no doubt traumatised by the severity of everything he saw: '...it is in most places, so waste, solitary, unpleasant and unsightly, so mute and still...that it striketh a certain horror.' This last remark was about the depth of Hell Gill, but it makes clear that the route across the bridge was in use from an early date.

Hell Gill marks the county boundary and the edge of the Yorkshire Dales National Park. The narrow neck of land lying between the gill, which later flows into the Eden and out to the Solway Firth, and the River Ure, which flows eastwards to the North Sea, lies on the watershed of Britain, the true divide between east and west.

To return to Appersett, start by retracing your steps for a few strides, and then branch left across an expanse of limestone pavement.

The track you are now taking is known as The High Way, and is part of the route taken by Lady Anne Clifford, one of the most renowned noblewomen of the

Stuart era, as she travelled between her Westmorland castles and estates. Once this was the major route through the valley from Hawes to Kirkby Stephen, and was in use until the 1820s when the new turnpike road (now the B6259) was built.

As it heads south-eastward, the High Way takes a slightly rising course. Before long it reaches High Hall, formerly an inn called the Highway House, on a well-used route through the mountains – well used, not only by nobility, but also by drovers, tradespeople, and highwaymen, too. And Mary Queen of Scots is said to have passed along it in 1568, on her way from Carlisle to imprisonment in Bolton Castle.

Passing for the most part alongside walls and along the steep edge of the escarpment, with a fine view of the valley, the route eventually rounds Cotter End, from where it descends to meet the road. Continue down the road for about 800yds/m, and then leave it, on the right, for a footpath that immediately crosses the river and rejoins your outward route for the final stage back to Appersett.

15 Cotterdale

The peaceful valley of Cotterdale lies between the mass of Great Shunner Fell and Lunds Fell, the source of the River Ure. At the confluence of West Gill and East Gill stands the small hamlet of Cotterdale, formerly, but rather grandly, called Cotterdale Town. Beyond the village, the waters combine into Cotterdale Beck, once known as the River Cotter. This walk travels into the valley on the north side of its beck, then crosses the snout of Cotter End and the River Ure, following the course of the latter back to Appersett.

Distance: 7 miles/11km
Height gain: 820ft/250m
Walking time: 3-4 hours
Type of walk: Moderate

hill walking, mainly on good paths
Start/Finish: Appersett. GR858907

In spite of being so close to the bustle of Hawes, Cotterdale is one of the less well known dales. That may well be because only one road enters and leaves the valley, prohibiting through traffic and discouraging run-of-the-mill curiosity. Cotterdale has only had the one road since early times, when the valley was occupied by three principal families – the Halls, the Kirks and the Kings – and gave rise to the couplet: 'Three halls, two kirks, and a king, Same road out as goes in'.

Walk out from Appersett on the Sedbergh road and cross the bridge spanning Widdale Beck. A short way on leave the road over a ladder stile on the left, and go right, alongside a wall, until you approach New Bridge, which crosses the River Ure. Cross the bridge and follow the road for the short distance to the Hardraw turning and at the junction cross to a stile (signposted for Bluebell Hill). Through the stile cross the ensuing field to a wall gap, and from there ascend obliquely left to a gate on the skyline above.

Continue ascending and strike across hill pasture to a ladder stile near a wall junction in the distance. Over the stile walk beside a wall until you emerge on an enclosed, broad, stony, track ascending left on to Great Shunner Fell; the track is part of the Pennine Way, and is now followed uphill for a while.

At a gate at a wall junction, you break out of the enclosed track onto open hill pasture, continuing along the Pennine Way until you reach a fingerpost on the left and a path branching to Cotterdale. A path sweeps across the hillside to a ladder stile over a wall, and then continues in much the same vein across hill slopes.

Across the valley rise the great mounds of Widdale Fell, Dodd Fell Hill and Drumaldrace, also known as Wether Fell. These are the fells that share the responsibility of harbouring Hawes, and are crossed by two important routes: one is an earlier stretch of the Pennine Way, which rises onto Dodd Fell Hill at Kidhow Gate and

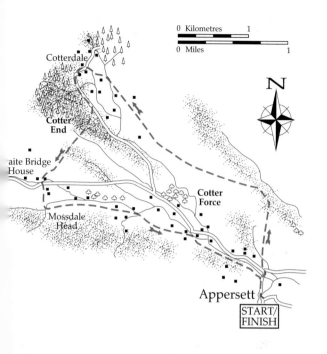

skirts along above Widdale; the other is Cam High Road, the Roman road that links Ingleton with their fort at Bainbridge.

Eventually the path runs on to meet a group of semi-collapsed sheep enclosures and then shortly reaches a metal gate, before continuing through a series of walled pastures. Keep going until you reach a waymark post in mid-field, directing you left to go down to a gated gap stile in a wall.

Through this, turn right, now about a quarter of a mile from Cotterdale. Go obliquely left down-field to a gate in the far bottom corner. Go forward beside a small stream and across three fields to reach a gate giving onto a footbridge spanning Cotterdale Beck.

Over the bridge turn left on a surfaced lane and follow this through the hamlet and out towards the main valley until you cross a cattle grid and can then leave the lane a short distance on, branching right on a footpath signposted for Thwaite Bridge. The path rises left onto rough hill pasture, and goes over Cotter End, crossing two walls by ladder stiles, and then descends on a waymarked path to a ladder stile at a wall corner. The descending path then goes down to reach Thwaite Bridge.

Cross the bridge and the main road and go over a stile opposite to climb beside a wall. When the wall bears left, at its high point, break away from it, keeping on in the same direction to cross to another wall. When this ends turn left and go down to a gate and cross a bridge spanning Mossdale Beck, with the attractive Mossdale Force just to the right.

Go between the first two buildings beyond the bridge and bear right to a gate. Aim half-left across the next field to a wooden gate, and then keep on walking roughly parallel with Mossdale Beck and, shortly, the River Ure, across several fields. The on-going route is waymarked whenever it needs to be, and is otherwise obvious, and eventually it leads to swing out to meet the A684. Just before it does so, leave the track, on the right, through a small gate, on a footpath for Appersett.

Walk forward along a field edge, beside a wall, to a gate and then across the next pasture to rejoin the River Ure. As you approach the river, cross a small in-flowing stream on the right and climb through banked woodland to a stile at the top. Over the stile, go left and walk beside a wall along the top edge of the woodland. An intermediate wall is crossed by a gap stile, from which a path runs on to a ladder stile in the distance.

The path continues along the top edge of woodland, and when this ends it descends to a stile on the river bank once more, and then continues alongside a wall parallel with the river. It finally runs on to meet New Bridge. Turn right as you reach the bridge and walk towards Appersett on your outward route.

16 Dodd Fell Hill and Drumaldrace

Acting as a kind of sleeping policemen between the upper reaches of Wharfedale and the much smaller valley of Raydale, Dodd Fell Hill and Drumaldrace, known also as Wether Fell, rise to the south of Hawes, and provided an obvious high-ground route for Roman surveyors. Later, the designers of the Pennine Way found the temptation of the Roman road irresistible. This walk examines the handiwork of both.

Distance: 12½ miles/ 20km
Height gain: 1,670ft/ 510m
Walking time: 4½-5½ hours
Type of walk: Good and easy walking on clear paths throughout. Long, but not over-demanding
Start/Finish: Dales Countryside Museum car park, Hawes. GR876899

This walk, though long, provides easy walking high above the dales and extensive panoramas that reach north-westwards to the blue-purple peaks of Lakeland. Beginning by reversing a stretch of the Pennine Way, the walk then circles back to Hawes along Cam High Road, a Roman highway, looping around Wether Fell before speeding down to reach Wensleydale once more at the village of Burtersett.

Start from the car park near the Dales Countryside Museum, where the station used to be. Leave the car park and walk out to the main road, cross it and follow the one-way system into Hawes. Just after passing the entrance to St Margaret's Church, go left through an alleyway (signposted 'Footpath to Gayle: Pennine Way'). This takes you up a flagged pathway beside the church to reach a squeeze stile beyond which a flagged path runs

out across fields above gurgling Gayle Beck to reach the minor road at Gayle.

On reaching the road go left for a short distance to a Pennine Way signpost on the right, and there leave the road for a pathway between houses. Cross an estate road and keep ahead to another stile, after which a flagged path leads left across a field to meet another lane.

Turn right, and follow the lane as it threads past cottages and farm buildings, rising a little to a footpath sign for the Pennine Way at a stile on the left. Through the stile, keep forward along a field edge, crossing an intermediate wall, before turning right through yet another stile a little way on. A green path now leads across fields to a quiet lane.

When the lane is reached, turn right, and left again in a few strides along the access to Gaudy Farmhouse. As the entrance to the farmhouse is reached, leave the access by a stile on the left, and take to a rising grassy path beside a wall. Follow this, ever onwards and upwards, at a leisurely pace, with the view across the dale below improving with height to take in the sprawl of Great Shunner Fell and Lovely Seat separated by the Buttertubs Pass.

For a while the modest gradient eases as the path swings right to round the base of Ten End, the northern edge of Dodd Fell Hill, and then rises again across a grassy shoulder to meet a track ascending from the dale below. Keep forward now on an obvious track (West Cam Road) to be guided by walls in various stages of disrepair all the way to Kidhow Gate, where a surfaced lane is encountered.

Long before then, anyone wanting to 'bag' Dodd Fell Hill can leave the Pennine Way soon after a wall, on the left, bends through ninety degrees. From hereabouts an untracked ascent can be made of this boggy summit. There is no right of way, but considerate walkers have been tolerated for many years. From the summit strike west, descending across difficult ground to rejoin the Pennine Way.

As you progress along the main route each of Yorkshire's 'Three Peaks' comes into view; first Whernside, then the unmistakable form of Ingleborough, and, as the signpost at Kidhow Gate is finally spotted ahead, Pen y Ghent looms across the intervening fells.

Go through Kidhow Gate, and pursue the surfaced Cam High Road, a route that linked forts at Ribblehead and Bainbridge. The long stroll that ensues flows along high above Langstrothdale and the infant waters of the River Wharfe until, on the rim of the steep descent into Sleddale, the Roman road branches right at a signpost indicating that the route is a byway to Bainbridge. Go right along it, and when a bridleway sign is reached at the end of a wall, and near the top of Wether Fell, ignore it, and keep ahead on the Roman road. Here the road rides high above Raydale and the blue expanse of Semerwater.

When a wall re-appears on the left, go through it on a signposted bridleway that leads out across rough pasture. Eventually this descends to meet another, more pronounced bridleway, which is followed downwards on a long and unmistakable line that leads unerringly to the village of Burtersett. As you descend into Burtersett, so you reach a road junction at a signpost pointing left to Gayle. Ignore this, and go right, following the main village road as it curves left and down between cottages.

Burtersett is a charming place, one of a number of hamlets in the Dales with names ending in 'sett', a clear indication that this was formerly a Norse settlement, for the ending comes from 'saetr' and means a hill farm or pasture. There was a settlement here, too, during the reign of Edward I (1272-1307), when the village had a forest lodge.

Go down through the village, and after the last houses leave the lane at a signposted footpath on the left (Hawes and Gayle), heading out across a field to another stile and gate beyond which a flagged pathway leads across a succession of fields, heading for Hawes, to reach a lane. Go left at the lane, and then immediately right, through more stiles to continue the flagged way to the edge of Hawes, at the A684. This busy road is now followed, left, for the short distance back into Hawes.

17 Hardraw Force

If all you want to do is see Hardraw Force, then simply go to the village and pay the entry fee. This walk, however, takes a rather circuitous approach, preferring to wander out to the secluded hamlet of Sedbusk and across the high slopes above Hardraw, before finally condescending to visit the falls. And a splendid sight they are, too, and most formidable after prolonged wet weather.

Distance: *7 miles/11km*
Height gain: *1,050ft/320m*
Walking time: *4 hours*
Type of walk: *A fine,* *varied walk with good views*
Start/Finish: *Hawes national park car park. GR875898*

Leave the car park along the path by the nearby railway bridge. The area now used as a car park used to be a railway goods yard on the Wensleydale line. There have been occasional rumblings about reopening parts of the old line, and it would be nice to see steam trains plying their way through the valley once more; but maybe that's just a pipe dream.

Turn right onto the road for about 100yds/m, and then leave it, on the left, for a flagged pathway across a corner of a field. Here you are on a brief stretch of the Pennine Way, which rejoins the road a short distance further on. Follow the road, which soon crosses the River Ure, and soon leave it again, this time on the right, at a stile from which a path rises gently north-east across fields, crossing a small arched bridge on the way, to meet a lane.

Cross the lane and a stile opposite and continue climbing, ultimately quite steeply, to a field corner stile giving onto the lane leading, right, into Sedbusk.

Sedbusk is a delightful place, a small hamlet of cottages and farms, with a grandstand view across the valley to Wether Fell and Dodd Fell Hill. Its name means 'the bush near the shieling', and from the edge of Hawes you can see it perched on the hillside like a place half-forgotten.

Follow a lane between the cottages and bear right at a small green, beyond which the lane becomes a rough track, Shutt Lane, built as an access to quarries, lead mines and lime kilns. This climbs now onto the fellside above until, just before reaching a gate, you can leave it, on the left, at a stile. From the stile a clear path continues the climb, turns a little indistinctly as it passes a small plantation, passes through two gates, and then assumes a more northerly course as it negotiates the eastern end of High Clint.

Having risen onto a more level moorland plateau, the path now swings round westward to head for the highest point of the walk, a large cairn with a splendid view, just off the main path.

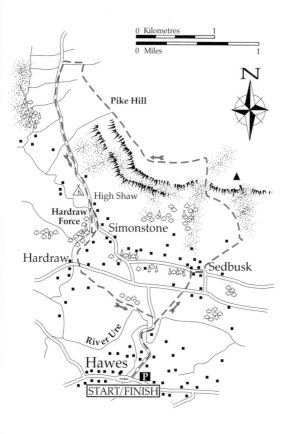

Although the scenery hereabouts has a fine distinctive character, it forms part of the much vaster Lovely Seat, the high point of Abbotside Common, which rises wetly to the north.

From High Clint the path heads north-west, but soon deteriorates. Keep on in the same direction to cross Pike Hill, and by maintaining a more or less level course you eventually intercept Shivery Gill, which you'll find is aptly named if you get caught up here in winter. Cross the gill and on the other side turn left down a track to the Buttertubs road. Follow the road downhill for some distance until you reach the first buildings at High Shaw.

Below, in a wooded ravine, Foss Beck is gathering strength for the mighty plunge that will soon follow. You have a choice here. Either continue down the road for another 400yds/m, or, from High Shaw go down a lane signposted to Fossdale. If you opt for the latter, you will soon go down steps into the wooded ravine, which has a few small waterfalls. Follow the beck downstream, on either bank, to a footbridge from which you turn up to rejoin the road.

Only a short way further down the road, having rejoined the more direct route, leave it, on the right, over a stile beside a gate. A track leads down to West House Farm, where you cross a stile on the right and go down two ensuing fields to reach Hardraw.

To visit the falls, however, you need to dig into your pocket because they are on private land, accessible through the nearby Green Dragon inn, admission to which is on payment of a small fee. It's certainly a worthwhile experience.

Hardraw Force is said to have the highest single drop of

any waterfall in England, and has long been a visitor attraction. W. Riley, writing in 'The Yorkshire Pennines of the North-West' in 1934 says: 'Like a merry schoolboy the Foss Beck comes romping down the woods from its birthplace on the heights of Great Shunner Fell, and leaps rather than falls over a ledge of hard rock into a deep pool, a hundred feet below.' He goes on to point out that if there has been prolonged dry weather, then the schoolboy is 'a very slim fellow', but that after rain, the falls are 'a miniature Niagara'. The Wordsworths came this way in 1799, and described the falls as 'lofty and magnificent', as indeed they are. Since the falls launch themselves clear of the overhanging lip over which they drop, it is feasible to walk behind them, but the rock is very slippery and such an antic is not advised.

To return to Hawes you once more make use of a stretch of the Pennine Way. From the inn, head towards a signposted track just to the left of the bridge. Go behind a group of buildings and left to a gate, and then strike across a number of fields to meet a road. Turn right and soon rejoin your outward route, and you can retrace your steps to Hawes.

18 Hawes West

This brief walk around the countryside to the west of Hawes is ideal for anyone with a few hours to spare. It touches on the River Ure, wanders across to the edge of Widdale and returns to encounter the Pennine Way at the neighbouring village of Gayle. It is ideal for an afternoon or evening stroll, perhaps at the start of a week's walking around Hawes.

Distance: *3 miles/5km*
Height gain: *Nominal*
Walking time: *2 hours*
Type of walk: *Easy*

walking through farm fields
Start/Finish: *Hawes. GR872898*

Leave Hawes by going past the Hawes Craft and Gift Centre at the rear of the Fountain Hotel. Go forward through a gate and along a narrow, walled, gravel path. When this emerges at a rough track, turn right and go through a gate and down another brief, walled track, turning left to cross a sloping pasture.

In the next field, keep on in the same direction alongside the old railway line and then go under a railway bridge through the centre of which there is a wall. On the other side, go left past two barns and across two fields, and in the second field be guided by a fenceline on the left to a gap stile in the distance, close by the banks of the River Ure. Go forward in the next pasture, with a fence on your right, and walk out to meet the main road. Turn left and follow the road for about 200yds/m until you can leave it, on the right, through a gate at Thorns, and along a footpath for Appersett Viaduct.

Go up the track to pass in front of the farm at Thorns, bearing right after the last building and walking round in a semicircle by a wall. Pass above a small stream before heading across a pasture to a gap stile near a gate.

Through the stile go half-right beside, but not across, another stream, towards a group of trees in a corner, and go into the next field. Follow a grassy path, with a wall on your left. In the field that follows head across towards a barn beside which there is a stile. Over the stile, head for another barn and then go half left across the next field towards a limekiln in the far corner.

Cross a nearby stile and then go forward with a fenceline on your left. When the fence ends keep forward up a slight rise, and bear slightly right on a path that goes through a wall gap. The path descends across the next field to a gate and goes on to reach Thorney Mire House. A ladder stile gives access to the house, and a waymark on it directs you ahead beside buildings to reach a lane. Turn left and go round a bend to discover that a footpath sign suggests that the right of way goes immediately in front of the house!

Follow the lane to the next bend and there leave it, going left on a bridleway, a broad, green, walled track that widens progressively, a clear path running throughout its length. At the end, the track bears right, before descending left to meet a road. Turn left for 40yds/m, and then leave the road, on the right, at a signposted footpath for Gayle. Go forward aiming to the right of a ruined barn, and cross a nearby wall. Bear half right across more fields to reach a lane at a gated gap stile. At the lane turn right and descend for a short distance, leaving it, on the left, at another stile reached by a small flight of steps.

Go half-right, down-field, leaving the field at another stile and walking across to a metal gate. Through this go along a muddy track to pass to the right of a barn. Turn left around the barn and follow a wall to a gap stile. In the next field follow a paved path, now almost entirely overgrown with grass, to reach a stile at the rear of Rookhurst Hotel, and then go up a rough ginnel to a lane where the Pennine Way is encountered. Turn left for 30yds/m and go through a stile and then on across more paved paths to reach the housing estate at Gayle. Pass between the houses to the main road, and turn left.

Gayle and Hawes today are almost inseparable, and share a rather haphazard manner of development. Many of the people of Gayle were descendants of the traditional Gayle knitters, who once had a prosperous cottage industry here, as indeed was common throughout the Dales. The two places were not always good neighbours, however, and history records a certain amount of rivalry, perhaps because both places shared the same industry. They both made cottons and, later, woollen yarns, until the conversion of corn mills to spinning brought about a decline in domestic knitting. Hawes later turned to making horse blankets and rugs, and towards the end of the 19th century housed the first Wensleydale cheese factory.

After 50yds/m leave the road, on the right, still following the Pennine Way, and walk along a paved path that leads to the rear of St Margaret's Church in Hawes. Walk down beside the church to conclude the walk.

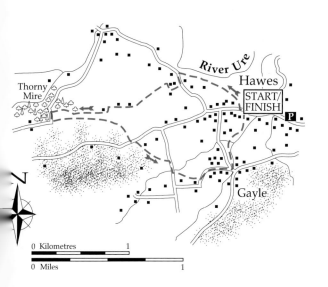

19 Skell Gill

The hamlet of Skell Gill is little more than a farm and a few cottages clustered around an old packhorse bridge. It's all fairly quiet and tranquil now, but this used to be a busy spot. The packhorse bridge alone tells you that it lies on a trade route, and all around on the moors lies evidence of a mining past. The old road that passes through the hamlet is a continuation of the High Way used by Lady Anne Clifford, here linking Hardraw and Askrigg.

Distance: 5¼ miles/ 8.5km	**Type of walk:** *A gentle pastoral stroll*
Height gain: *375ft/115m*	**Start/Finish:** *Bainbridge. GR934902*
Walking time: *3 hours*	

Bainbridge is a delightful, welcoming place of sturdy houses, shops and pubs built around an elongated green, the manorial rights over which were granted to the people of Bainbridge in 1663, and managed by the Lords Trustees of the Manor of Bainbridge.

The village sits beside the River Bain, Yorkshire's shortest river, which from its source in Semerwater joins the River Ure just north of the village. The course of the Bain is quite steep, and so the river is invariably lively. Camden noted "...a little River coming out of the South called Baint, which with a greate noise streameth out of the Poole Semer".

The oldest part of Bainbridge is at the southern end, where the houses seem to have been built in a haphazard manner. Close by, the river chatters over its limestone bed, making a few miniature falls as it flows under the bridge that gives the village its name.

To the east, overlooking the village, Brough Hill is the site of a Roman fort, Virosidum, which, appropriately, means 'high seat'. It lies at one end of a road extending westward to Ingleton, and was built as part of the process of pacifying the Brigantes, who inhabited this region. The road was probably constructed during the time of Petillius Cerialis, but it was Agricola who completed the pacification and built many of the forts, including that at Brough Hill, though his fort was later replaced with one of stone construction. It remained garrisoned until the end of the 4th century, and although it has been recorded as a prominent feature since Camden's day, it was not until the 1920s that it was significantly excavated.

Begin the walk by heading north along the road to Yore Bridge – Yore being an early name for the Ure. Yorebridge House, close by the bridge, was formerly the grammar school, adjoined by the headmaster's house.

Having crossed the bridge, go through a stile on the left and cross the old railway, soon reaching Yorescott Farm, beyond which you meet the road again. Turn left for a little over 100yds/m, then leave the road, on the right, for a footpath (signposted to Skell Gill). Off to the right you can see Coleby Hall, a 17th-century manor house.

The on-going path descends first to cross Meer

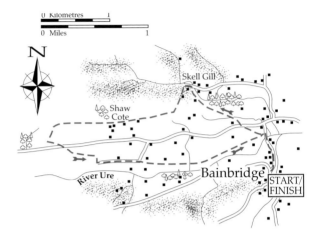

Beck, then climbs gently to meet the course of Skellgill Beck before finally reaching the hamlet. Here, turn left, passing cottages, and then go left again just before reaching a ford onto a track. Now the track sweeps roughly westward across Cote Pasture, serving four farms in the space of a little over a mile (2km) of what for walkers is invigorating stuff.

Finally, you meet a walled lane that shortly curves southward and, beyond a gate, heads down to the road. Cross the road and descend through limestone outcrops, some of which have been quarried. Keep descending until you hit more level ground, and a track heading east past Old Cams House. Beyond, you meet a lane. Follow this until it turns sharply left, and then take to a path that follows the course of the dismantled valley railway, which will guide you back to Yore Bridge, from where you retrace your steps into Bainbridge.

20 Askrigg and Worton Scar

This brief walk visits three attractive villages in the dale, and samples both sides of the river. Everywhere the scenery is lovely, and in spring and early summer, when Nature is alive and shouting at you from every field, every hedgerow and every treetop, it is a most rewarding and satisfying experience.

Distance: *4 miles/6.5km*
Height gain: *260ft/80m*
Walking time: *2-2½ hours*

Type of walk: *Gentle walking on good paths*
Start/Finish: *Bainbridge. GR934902*

Most of what I have to say about Bainbridge I covered in Walk 19, which also begins from the village, except to add that so lovely is Bainbridge that there are days when you can sit on one of the benches overlooking the green, watching the world go by, and really not get going at all. This is calendar material, and immensely popular as a result; but you can still find quiet moments during the year.

To begin, go along the road to Yore Bridge, and on the other side go across a field on a flagged pathway, crossing the course of the former railway and a small stone bridge spanning a tributary before reaching the hamlet of Grange.

Grange is where the first monastery in Wensleydale, Fors Abbey, was sited. King Stephen was on the throne when the abbey was founded in 1145, and for eleven years the monks eked a living from a countryside that was rather less hospitable than today's. Their leader, Peter de Quincey, was from the abbey of Savigny in Brittany, but the Abbot of Savigny was not happy that such a wild setting had been chosen for the abbey on the Ure, and in due course placed it under the jurisdiction of the 'Abbot of Joreval', or Jervaulx, as we know it today.

At Grange, you meet a road. Turn right along this for about 80yds/m and then leave it, branching left onto a path across fields to the footbridge at Mill Gill. Cross the footbridge and go past a mill, and along the lane into Askrigg.

The village of Askrigg seems to be surrounded by low glacial hillocks, and its main street is steep and winding in a delightful fashion. It is a place that is always refreshing to visit, no matter how many times you do so, and you do so always with anticipation. It has some of the feel of a small town, but none of the drawbacks, seeming to repose gracefully against the fells and amid the lush meadows, as if content to let time and the world go by.

It has certainly been here a long time, and used to be on the edge of a great medieval hunting forest. Later its strategic position helped it to develop as a small market town, and many of its houses date from the heyday of commercial activity in the 17th and 18th centuries.

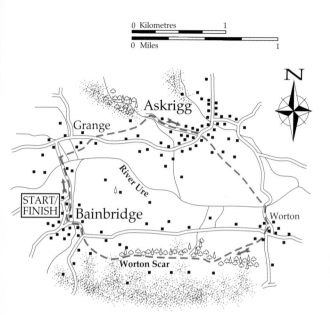

Go into the road opposite the market cross, passing cottages and, ignoring a walled lane, going forward through a field and crossing the old railway line once more. This pathway, too, is flagged, and leads eventually to the hamlet of Worton (pronounced Werton). Here you will find one of the oldest buildings left in the dale, the mullion-windowed farmhouse of Worton Hall.

Go through Worton and up to the main valley road, and there turn right for a few strides before going left, through a gate. A good path leads across a field, onto Worton Scar, a slender strip of woodland. Turn right along the scar, which in springtime is bright with wild flowers and loud with birdsong; occasionally, too, you may spot a roe deer, though I confess I've not seen them here myself.

As you walk along the scar, you move onto Brough Scar, and benefit from an improving view of the Roman fort on Brough Hill. And then it's quickly downhill to the road and back into Bainbridge.

21 Whitfield Gill Force

Waterfalls seem to abound on this short walk from Askrigg, and the spectacle of them is therefore enlivened after rain. But other themes also flow through the walk: there are good examples of glacial deposits around Askrigg, medieval cultivation terraces – lynchets – and the ever-present trail of Lady Anne Clifford. Add to that the fascination that is Askrigg itself, and you have a small but very potent walk of great character and interest. Geologists, botanists and nature lovers, too, will have a field day here.

Distance: *3 miles/4.5km*
Height gain: *425ft/130m*
Walking time: *2½ hours*
Type of walk: *An easy*
walk, suitable for everyone
Start/Finish: *Askrigg.*
GR948910

You begin from the market cross in Askrigg by heading along a lane through West End, near the church. At the end of the lane, go across a pasture towards what used to be a sawmill. Cross a nearby footbridge, and then turn right, along the course of wooded Mill Gill. Soon, you must follow a diverging path if you want to see the Mill Gill falls, a most attractive cascade flowing in steps created by the local Yoredale rocks; at least three different types of rock can be seen here – limestone, sandstone and shale.

Return to the main route and follow a signposted path to the scattered group of cottages at Helm.

There is strong evidence, some of it deduced by that renowned and reliable authority on Dales' subjects, Geoffrey Wright – who used to live in Helm – that the hamlet lies on the continuation of Lady Anne Clifford's High Way. This remarkable woman (her story most vividly told in Richard Spence's 1997 book 'Lady Anne Clifford') was High Sheriff of Westmorland, and travelled extensively through this region, often with a massive retinue, going about her business, and often proving to be something of a thorn in Oliver Cromwell's side.

Near Helm, you meet the end of Skellgill Lane. Here turn right, heading up through the hamlet, and then continue climbing until you can bear right to reach the gill once more, in a wooded ravine. You'll find a footbridge here, but before heading for it go up the left-hand side of the ravine, following a signposted path for Whitfield Force, properly Whitfield Gill Force. Gradually, the path descends to the falls, which, like those lower down, are quite splendid.

Whitfield Gill is an attractive example of a gill wood, and you can expect to find quite a range of trees here from beautiful beeches – which are native to Britain, but do not occur naturally north of the Cotswolds, although these in the gill may well be self-sown; their predecessors will have been planted – to holly, rowan, oak, larch, ash and hawthorn.

Go back to the footbridge and cross the gill to go up

to reach Low Straights Lane. Now simply follow the lane until it meets the road north of Askrigg, and turn right to return. Or, just before reaching a ford at Askrigg Beck, you can turn right and go down through numerous fields to the village. As you go down through the fields keep an eye open for those lynchets, medieval cultivation terraces intended to improve the drainage and quality of the ground.

22 Semerwater

This delightful walk wanders easily across hillsides above the River Bain to the bright-eyed spread of Semerwater, before climbing high onto the moors to join the Roman road.

Distance: *8 miles/13km*   *strenuous in places; not*
Height gain: *985ft/300m*   *advised in poor visibility*
Walking time: *4 hours*   **Start/Finish:** *Bainbridge.*
Type of walk: *Fairly*   *GR934902*

Start from the village green in Bainbridge and walk out on the Leyburn road. After a short distance uphill, just by a lay-by, leave the road for a footpath on the right signposted to Semerwater. The path climbs to run alongside a wall before branching away across hillside pastures, on a signposted footpath that leads ultimately to a wall with two, gated, gap stiles.

Take the stile on the right and follow a green path over a slight rise and then descend to a wall corner. Then follow a path running beside the wall. Cross more hill pastures until you descend to a ladder stile. Having crossed the stile, follow a green path beside the River Bain until you reach Semerwater Bridge.

Semerwater is a product of the last Ice Age, though it is today only a puddle of its former self, which dammed the whole valley.

This is the prosaic version; legend provides something much more dramatic. Here, it is said, an angel came one day disguised as a beggar, seeking food and shelter, but was turned away by everyone in the village, until, at last, the angel came to a ramshackle hut set a distance from the rest. Here the man and his wife invited the stranger in, and willingly shared their meagre possessions. The next morning, the angel, being in a vengeful mood, turned towards the village below, and brought forth great torrents from the hillsides that flooded the village and drowned all its inhabitants, save for the man and his wife, who were saved. Just along the road from Semerwater Bridge stands Low Blean, which is said to be the house of the hospitable couple.

From more recent times comes the tradition, introduced in the 1960s, of an open-air service performed on August Bank Holiday Sunday, by the vicar of Askrigg and Stalling Busk, from a boat on the lake. A large congregation is usually in attendance, and the Hawes Brass Band accompanies the hymns. Not even poor weather deflects the occasion, except to allow the vicar to conduct the service from the safety of the lakeshore.

Go over the bridge, as if heading to nearby Countersett, where George Fox stayed in 1677, and in a few strides leave the road for a footpath on the left signposted to Marsett Lane. The path crosses a number of fields to meet the lane at a step stile. Turn left and follow the lane for about 500yds/m

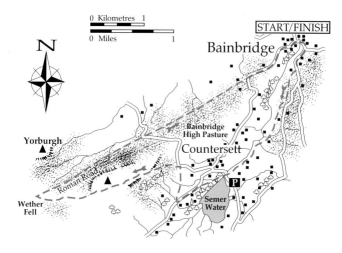

until you descend to a footpath on the right for Countersett and Crag Side Road.

Turn onto the footpath and follow it towards farm buildings, climbing to the right of a stream to a gated gap stile. In the next pasture, climb obliquely right to another stile in the top right-hand corner of the pasture. Head diagonally right up-field towards a power line pole near a dilapidated wall corner, and there bear right to a gap stile and left to cross the corner of a hill pasture and climb to a ladder stile above, giving onto Crag Side Road.

You immediately leave the road through a gate on the left to pursue a broad track (signposted to Wether Fell). Follow the rising track to a gate and through the gate bear left to another gate, and then rising beyond on a green track.

The track takes you up onto the moorland top and forward through two gates/stiles, pressing on across the moor top to intersect a footpath (signposted), near which another signpost points the way forward to the 'Roman road'.

Keep on in the same direction until you meet the broad, stony track of Cam High Road, the Roman road between Ingleton and Bainbridge. When you do, turn right and follow in the footsteps of legionnaires all the way back to the outskirts of Bainbridge. At Four Lane Ends you cross a surfaced road linking Burtersett and Countersett.

Cam High Road sweeps on downhill across Bainbridge High Pasture to rejoin the Countersett road on the edge of Bainbridge. Now simply follow the surfaced road down into Bainbridge.

23 Aysgarth and Ivy Scar

There is much crammed into this pleasant walk, from the beauty and drama of the Aysgarth Falls and the River Ure to the high moorland pastures below Ivy Scar; it also manages to squeeze in a visit to the nearby village of Carperby before finally returning to Aysgarth. The riverside pastures are pure delight, while the views afforded by the moorland crossing are excellent and inspiring.

Distance: *6 miles/10km*
Height gain: *490ft/150m*
Walking time: *3-4 hours*
Type of walk: *Moderate dale and hill walk; best on*
a clear day
Start/Finish: *Aysgarth visitor centre car park. GR011888*

Aysgarth has Norman origins, though nothing survives from those early times; all is now comparatively modern. It is a popular place today, because of the splendid waterfalls that occur near the village, where, after a long and fairly quiet passage from the edge of the Vale of Eden, the River Ure starts to flex its muscles; it is an impressive sight. Much of the village's earlier importance stemmed from the fact that it was the parish for the whole of the upper dale. Of the church, which is built away from the village, and nearer to the river, only the lower part of the 12th-century tower remains; the rest is 19th century, but built in styles that reflect Early English and Perpendicular.

Start from the national park visitor centre in Aysgarth and walk through the car park to locate a path at the rear going left down towards the Upper Aysgarth Falls. Do not cross the road bridge, but keep forward on a track from which you can deviate, left, to view the falls. Return to the main track and turn left on a rising green path between fences. The path runs through woodland and then turns right to go between the abutments of the old railway line, and then, in the ensuing pasture, bears slightly left, past a pond to cross to a gap stile in a distant wall to the right of a farm.

Go past a tennis court and then, at a wall corner, turn left to cross a stile. In the next field go forward beside a wall and fence, and keep on in the same direction when the fence bends left, to reach a concealed gated gap stile giving onto a lane. Cross the lane, and in the next pasture follow the bottom field edge towards a gate on the skyline ahead. Pass through a stile near the gate, and then continue to follow a fence and then a wall to a wall junction to the right of which there is another stile. Through this, turn left and go down to another stile, after which bear left to a wall and shortly join the old railway trackbed.

When the trackbed path is deflected down steps to meet a lane, turn left and go down towards the

River Ure. After 100yds/m, turn right on a footpath alongside the river. Cross an in-flowing stream and then continue along the river bank.

The riverside path runs on for one and a quarter miles (2km) at varying distances from the river, and gradually moves to a step stile over a fence on the right. After the stile, turn right between the abutments of the old railway, and walk up to the main road at Woodhall.

At the main road cross into a rough lane opposite, rising onto fellsides below Ivy Scar. Climb to a fingerpost, where the track forks. Branch right to a gate. Through this turn right on a bridleway. The track runs on between walls heading for Ivy Scar, and wanders on easily to reach Disher Force. It then continues through a gate and across the open hill pasture of Ox Close.

A gravel track leads onto some old mine workings. As it bears left, leave it and go forward on a broad grassy track. Follow the green track to another bridleway signpost, and keep on in the same direction, rising gently, to meet a stile and gate in a wall. Through this bear right alongside the wall, which will guide you towards a vehicle track. Follow this through a gap, just beyond which the track forks. Here branch right, descending beside a stream and wall with the village of Carperby now in view in the valley below; likewise Aysgarth, more distant.

Follow the on-going track until it comes down to a

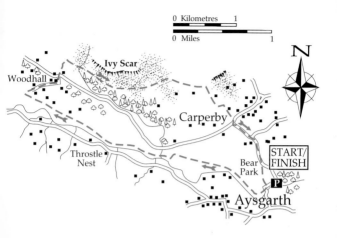

track junction, and here descend, slightly right, to go through a metal gate and down a vehicle track through an elongated pasture, heading towards Carperby. Keep on down through a gate and stile and then about 250yds/m later, leave the descending track through a gated gap stile on the left.

Cross to the far corner of the next field, and then go down another elongated pasture, which leads you to a farm. Go between farm buildings and cross a concrete track, keeping forward on a grassy, walled track, cluttered with farm rubbish, to the rear of cottages, and then bear left into the village.

Carperby was an important centre for the growth of the Quaker faith. The first meetings were held by Richard Robinson in 1659, and George Fox came here on his

preaching tours. A number of the villagers still have the
ancient woodland right of 'estover', or Assignment
Wood, that is, the right to gather firewood from
Freeholder's Wood near the falls.

Take the first turning on the right at the village
green, and go right again onto the Askrigg road a
short distance further on. After 100yds/m, branch
left on the road to Aysgarth Falls. About 40yds/m
after a turning (Low Lane) on the left, leave the
road at a stile on the right, and walk in the same
direction alongside a wall.

When you meet a green track entering through a
gate from the road, start moving away from the
wall, aiming for the right-hand edge of a small
group of trees. When you get there, go over a stile
beside a gate and across the next field to another
stile. Beyond this, a path leads to a kissing gate
giving access to the old railway trackbed. Over the
trackbed, steps lead down into the visitor centre
car park.

24 Aysgarth to Castle Bolton

This pleasant circuit from Aysgarth to the village of Castle Bolton and back is easy walking, and a delight at any time of year, though it is especially beautiful in spring, when many of the pastures are filled with new-born lambs. The ancient Bolton Castle, considered by Pevsner to be 'a climax of English military architecture', is an added pleasure, as is the village itself, probably laid out at the time the castle was built, and St Oswald's 14th-century church.

Distance: *6 miles/10km*
Height gain: *260ft/80m*
Walking time: *3 hours*
Type of walk: *Easy walking on field paths and tracks*
Start/Finish: *Aysgarth visitor centre car park. GR011888*

Begin from the national park visitor centre at Aysgarth by walking out to the road and following a fenced pathway to the right, shortly crossing the road and going through a gate on a path (signposted to Middle Falls and Lower Falls). The path takes you down into Freeholder's Wood, which is an ancient woodland where the national park authority has reintroduced traditional coppicing to regenerate the wood and provide wildlife habitats.

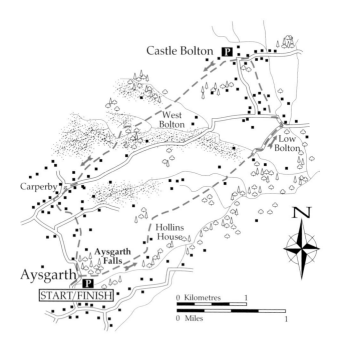

A brief diversion, right, down steps takes you to a viewing platform overlooking the Middle Falls; return to the main path and turn right, and press on to the Lower Falls. Another short deviation leads to these falls. On the way out, at a path junction, turn right and follow the on-going path above the river to a stile. Over this, walk forward, climbing beside an intermittent hedgerow on your left to meet a fence. Here turn right and walk beside the fence to a stile.

Cross the ensuing field in much the same direction,

but bearing slightly left towards Hollin House Farm. Go through the farmyard, and when you reach open pastureland keep forward a short distance before leaving the access, at a signpost, for a track bearing right to a stile in a distant wall.

In the pasture beyond go forward on a green track with Bolton Castle now in view ahead. The track guides you down to a wall and fence junction. Here cross a stile over a fence (do not go through the gap stile in the adjoining wall), and turn right on a rutted track, and follow the wall. Go over a step stile and a gap stile a few strides later, and then continue with the wall on your right. When the wall bends right, leave it and go forward on another green path that moves across to accompany a wall forward to enter the enclosed Thoresby Lane.

Follow the lane to Low Thoresby Farm, where the track becomes surfaced. Follow this around the farm and out to meet the road on the edge of Redmire. Turn left.

About 60yds/m after the road bends to the left, leave it, on the right, through a gap stile, and then follow an obvious green path across numerous fields linked by stiles. At one stage the path crosses the trackbed of the former Wensleydale Railway, before continuing into Castle Bolton.

When you reach the village, turn left and walk towards the castle.

The castle was built in 1379 for Richard de Scrope, Lord

Chancellor of England to Richard II. Today, this massive fortress is one of the best preserved in the country, and dominates the surrounding countryside it was built to defend.

Go forward past the church of St Oswald, with the castle on your left, and keep on along a broad track to pass a car park. Just after a gate across the track, leave it, and bear left to a gap stile in a field corner. Cross a small enclosure, and then from a wall corner descend obliquely across a wide, open pasture on a footpath signposted to Aysgarth.

On the far side, pass through the left-hand of two metal gates, and on across another pasture. In the third field, you descend to cross Beldon Beck by a footbridge, rising beyond to another stile. Then continue across fields to West Bolton Farm. Go directly in front of the farm buildings on its access track to locate a gated gap stile on the right. The on-going path passes to the north of a small plantation, and then goes on to cross a stream. Over the stream bear right to a stile, and then keep on along an obvious green track across a number of pastures.

The track eventually brings you down to pass another farm and meet the main road on the edge of Carperby. Turn right along the road into the village as far as the Wheatsheaf pub and turn left onto a footpath directly opposite (signposted to Aysgarth). Cross a stream to go into an elongated pasture, and go forward with a wall on your right. Pass a metal gate and then leave the pasture at a gap stile, on the right, about 150yds/m from the road. Through the stile, turn left, and walk beside a wall to reach Low Lane. Cross the lane to pass through a gap stile, and then go forward with a wall on your right. When the wall ends go through another stile, and then left across a number of fields on an obvious grassy path. The final gate and gap stile leads into the top edge of Freeholder's Wood. Follow a path through the wood, initially right and then descending left to a gate giving onto the road. Turn left and go beneath an old railway bridge, and immediately turn right to return to the visitor centre car park.

25 Addlebrough Moors

This excellent moorland walk effects a circuit of the prominent table-top fell of Addlebrough. There are outstanding views of the whole valley, but most stunning is the surprise one you get of Semerwater, set against the wild mass of Wether Fell. Since the main point of the walk is the benefit of elevation, from which to survey much of the dale, leave this route for a fine summer's day, and avoid it altogether in poor visibility.

Distance: 6¹/₂ miles/ 11km
Height gain: 740ft/225m
Walking time: 3-4 hours
Type of walk: Moderate

moorland walking
Start/Finish: Worton. GR958899. Lay-by opposite the pub on A684

Limited parking in Worton means that the best place to start is from a lay-by along the main road. So, walk back towards Worton and turn left at a crossroads up the steep lane to Cubeck. Turn into Cubeck, a small farming community, and continue up a walled track to a gate. Beyond the gate you cross a field, climbing quite steeply to another gate, at the top corner, where Addlebrough now comes into view. Head right, to another gate. Beyond this, the route follows a more level course for a while to yet another gate, before finally accompanying a wall to reach Carpley Green Road. Turn left.

The road skirts Addlebrough, and provides a grand view of Semerwater and Raydale. Just before a barn, go left through a gate, then follow a right-hand wall to another gate which gives into a large hill pasture devoid of prominent paths. Head across to a distant gate, beyond which lie the remains of what may well have been a Brigantian settlement. Go forward across two fields, and, from a gate in the right-hand wall, cross the next pasture to a stile, where you move out onto the bleak, open

expanse of Thornton Rust Moor.

Across the moor, another gate gives access to a small field, on the far side of which you go into a walled lane, which shepherds you down to the remote and tranquil village of Thornton Rust.

This is a delightful village in a splendid position on a rocky platform overlooking the valley. Essentially, it is one fairly wide street of cottages and farms, with the fells climbing away from it. The village, which unlike most of the dale developed as a Calvinistic stronghold, used to observe the custom, whenever anyone died, of ringing a bell at the centre and either end of the village, as an invitation to each family to send someone to attend the funeral.

Follow the lane as it zigzags down to the village, and then turn left to leave the village behind.

On the edge of the village, look for a gate on the right, signposted to Nipe End. From a stile below, you follow a path into a narrow strip of woodland soon to emerge into a field at a stile in a dilapidated wall. Now all that remains is to link a long and quick-fire succession of gap stiles down to the road. Turn left to return to the start.

26 West Witton Moor

This pleasant short walk wanders easily up onto the moors below Penhill, and makes an ideal outing for short winter days. Across the valley, the imposing Bolton Castle continues to dominate the landscape, as it has done for hundreds of years.

Distance: *4 miles/7km* **Height gain:** *690ft/210m* **Walking time:** *2-3 hours*	**Type of walk:** *Easy tracks and paths* **Start/Finish:** *West Witton. GR058884. Very limited parking.*

West Witton, a small road-edge settlement once the centre of a prosperous dyeing trade, looks northwards across the valley, and has its back to the protective escarpment of Penhill. A nearby farm called Chantry is a reminder that Jervaulx Abbey had a small chapel here from which its monks helped to guide travellers crossing Penhill to safety by firing a warning. There's still a church here, but a Victorian edifice replaced the old Norman church in 1875.

Leave West Witton by walking up the lane at the western end of the village at Kagram, and follow this as it climbs steadily. There is a fine view across the valley of Bolton Castle and its attendant village.

Still ascending on a surfaced lane, keep on past a caravan park, beyond which the lane (Green Gate) becomes gravelled and stony. It eventually levels and runs on to a track junction. Here, go forward through a metal gate, following a path onto West Witton Moor. A few strides on, when the track forks, branch left, and continue rising with it to a gate and stile. Beyond the gate the on-going track rises, left, towards a wall, and then reaches a more level plateau, below the craggy edges of Black Scar and Penhill Scar.

The green path leads up to a gate, and beyond this it continues left. When it forks, branch right, and when you reach the third collapsed wall crossed by the track, leave it, bearing left on an initially indistinct path to a gate/stile in a distant wall corner.

Through the stile turn right and walk alongside a wall to enter an enclosed track, Flint Lane, which wanders eastwards below the slopes of Penhill. When Flint Lane ends near Penhill Farm, at a surfaced lane, go forward a little and then turn left down a signposted footpath (Witton Bank). The descending path takes you across slopes that in spring are bright with wood anemone, early purple orchid and violet.

Go down through a wall and on a short distance further to rejoin the surfaced lane at a bend. Turn right and descend for about 300yds/m, and then leave the road on the left, either through a gated gap stile or along a parallel stony track, the first part of which is often running with water.

The footpath later joins the track at a gate and then goes forward past a ruined farmhouse. A walled green lane continues to another ruined building. Immediately after this, bear half right across a large pasture to a stile on the edge of a caravan site. Through the stile go down to cross a stream bridge, entering the caravan site along a rising gravel track between static caravans. Just as the track bends left, leave it, on the right, along a short, fenced track to a gate at the top edge of woodland. Go down through the woodland to meet a lane, and turn right to retrace your outward steps to West Witton.

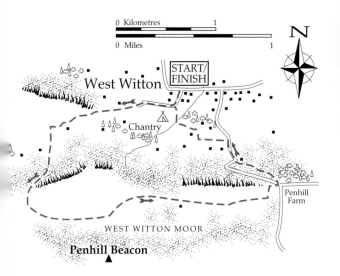

27 Redmire Force

While working on this book, I was blessed with some fine spring weather. As a result I had to make three attempts to complete this walk, simply because the beauty of the riverside path in particular – it must be the finest stretch of the Ure – invoked a great reluctance to move on, and had film almost buzzing through the cameras. The walk visits a chapel of the Knights Templar, historic, but not over-interesting, though Bolton Hall, set in splendid parkland across the river, is quite another matter. It has been the home of succeeding lords of Bolton for at least 300 years.

Distance: *6¹/₄ miles/ 10km*	**Type of walk:** *Easy walking on good paths*
Height gain: *575ft/175m*	**Start/Finish:** *West Witton. GR063884*
Walking time: *3-4 hours*	

West Witton is a linear village, its houses hung out along the village street like clothes on a washing line. Originally, the houses, mostly 19th century, were the homes of lead miners, though there are still a few which date earlier than this.

Head east out of West Witton and almost immediately take walled Back Lane on the left. When this forks, branch right, and descend towards the river. At the end of the lane, take the right-hand one of two gates, and then turn along the left-hand boundary wall, following this as it winds down to another gate, now close by the river. Go through the gate and cross a nearby stream, then descend to another gate in a fence to the right.

Now you join the river bank, which here forms the boundary of the national park. Follow the river upstream, passing through a number of pastures until you approach a large wooded island. Here a wall appears, and deflects you away from the river. Follow the wall, cross a stile and the ensuing field to another stile concealed in a corner. From there, a better path leads through trees to a grandstand view of Redmire Force. The force is not so impressive as others in the dale, but is nonetheless an attractive and pleasing sight.

As soon as you reach the falls, climb steps away from the river, and leave the woods at a stile, to cross another field. Continue in much the same direction, guided by a nearby wall until you meet a fence. Follow this for a while, until it turns sharply away, and then keep on in the same direction to a stile in a wall corner. Beyond, you descend to touch on the river again, but soon enter a large pasture, where the wall turns away.

Follow the wall and soon enter walled Stony Stoop Lane, which leads you up to meet the main road. Turn left along the road until, just before Temple Farm, you encounter a roadside temple built in the 18th century by the owners of Swinithwaite Hall. Here you leave the road, by going over a stile on the right, and then follow a broad track to the top of the ensuing field, where there is a gate. Beyond the gate you ascend through a small woodland, at the top edge of which a stile gives access to the site of the chapel of the Knights Templar.

The Knights Templar were members of a medieval religious and military order officially named the Order of the Poor Knights of Christ. They were popularly known as the Knights of the Temple of Solomon, or Knights Templar, because their first quarters in Jerusalem adjoined a building known as Solomon's Temple. The order grew from a small military group started in Jerusalem in 1119 by two French knights, Hugh des Payens and Godfrey of St Omer, with the aim of protecting pilgrims visiting Palestine after the First Crusade.

The Knights Templar obtained papal approval of their order, and in 1128 were given an austere rule closely following that of the monastic order of Cistercians. After the last Crusades had failed and interest had waned in an aggressive policy against the Muslims, the Knights Templar were no longer needed. Meanwhile, their immense riches had aroused the envy of secular as well as ecclesiastical powers, and in 1307 the impoverished Philip IV of France, with the aid of Pope Clement V, arranged for the arrest of the French grand master Jacques de Molay on charges of sacrilege and Satanism. Molay and the leading officers of the order confessed under torture, and all of them were eventually burned at the stake. Five years later, the order was suppressed by Pope Clement V and its property assigned to the rival Knights Hospitaller, although most of it was in fact seized by Philip and by King Edward II, who disbanded the order in England.

From the chapel, a less pronounced path ensues, heading for a gate at the top of the next field, where, for a while, you follow a concrete farm access. When the access bends sharply right, leave it and head up to the top of the field to a wall corner. Here pass through a gate and go forward across two fields to reach Langthwaite Lane, an old green lane. This ancient highway will now steer you back to the edge of West Witton, and a surfaced lane descending into the village.

28 Walden

Rising south from the beautiful village of West Burton, the dale of Walden rises steadily to the squat mound of Buckden Pike. Of the many dales, most walkers, because West Burton itself is off the beaten track, overlook this one. But it is unquestionably a splendid dale. The route penetrates the dale on field paths above the west bank of Walden Beck, and then returns on the other side.

Distance: *6 miles/10km*	*walking on field paths*
Height gain: *490ft/150m*	**Start/Finish:** *West*
Walking time: *3 hours*	*Burton. GR018867*
Type of walk: *Easy*	

West Burton, a former market village, lies at the junction of Bishopdale and Walden, the two dales separated by the wedge of Wasset Fell. Rows of attractive houses and cottages rise alongside the elongated village green until you are led into Walden. And as you walk into the dale, so you are treated to a gradually unfolding landscape rather than handed the whole thing of beauty at the outset. Isolated farms dot partially plantationed hillsides, with a care over placement, sadly not much in evidence these days, which suggests their builders knew how to enhance a landscape.

Go up through the village of West Burton, passing the village green and the chapel, and turn left onto a rising lane (signposted 'Walden only'). When the lane forks, branch left for Walden South, and just

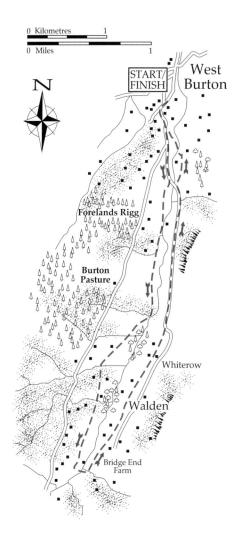

0 Kilometres 1

0 Miles 1

START/FINISH

West Burton

N

Forelands Rigg

Burton Pasture

Whiterow

Walden

Bridge End Farm

before reaching Cote Bridge, spanning Walden Beck, leave the lane, on the right, at a gap stile to go along a footpath signposted to Cowstone Gill.

Walk into the field, alongside a wall, to a gated gap stile on the left, which begins a long succession of fields and stiles. The way forward across the fields is never in doubt, though you do break out of the routine for a while as you cross through bracken onto open hillside pasture below the plantations of Burton Pasture, guided by waymark poles.

Strike across the next field and then cross a stream, and, having done so, bear right, going round a wall and keeping it on your left. Then climb slightly to another stile, and a few strides later cross a fence and turn left to follow the field edge to the top far corner (though the right of way shown on the map suggests a more direct route). Go over a step stile here and descend to a small gate. Beyond this, cross a stream, Cowstone Gill, by a footbridge and immediately turn right to a gated gap stile. A path takes you up to a signpost at the rear of a farm building. From the signpost, ignore the obvious access track and bear left on a grassy path across the ensuing field to a gate. Beyond the gate go forward alongside a wall towards Hargill Farm.

Keep to the right of the farmhouse, and walk on towards another signpost and a concealed gateway. Through the gate cross a stream and go up on the other side, forward past a barn and across to a stile, and then forward again across more pastures linked by gap stiles.

As you approach Bridge End Farm you cross a small stream and enter an ancient hay meadow. Follow the waymarked route across this to a vehicle track on the far side (do not shortcut to the farm). Turn left, going towards the farm, but before reaching it, bear right to a gap stile in a wall, overlooking Walden Beck.

Over the stile, go left to cross the beck by a bridge, and then immediately turn left. Cross a step stile about 40yds/m further on, and then rise obliquely right on a grassy path up to a gate. Through the gate turn left to begin the return journey to West Burton, alongside a wall and on a path that is higher than the outward journey and commands a much better view both up and down this delectable valley. When the wall bends left, keep on in the same direction to a derelict farmhouse, and then keep on across several pastures until you reach Whiterow Farm.

From the farm walk out along its access to meet Whiterow Road, and go down it until you reach Cote Bridge. Just before the bridge leave the road, on the right, along a footpath signposted to Ruckwith Bridge. Go forward between a wall and Walden Beck to a gate, and then forward alongside a wall and later a fence. When you reach a footbridge spanning Walden Beck, cross it and ascend the obvious path on the other side to reach the lane into West Burton. When you reach the lane turn right and walk back down into the village.

29 Leyburn and Wensley

Wensley is a most charming place of soft grey cottages surrounded by rolling green hillsides. It is a small village with a long history, and was the first town in the dale to have a market charter. Had it not been for the effects of the plague, which broke out here in the 16th century, Wensley might still be a more important place than neighbouring Leyburn, which has certainly exceeded it in size. This circular walk begins in Leyburn, treks across farm fields to Wensley, and then flirts with the River Ure as far as Middleham Bridge. A brief excursion to neighbouring Harmby precedes the final walk back into Leyburn.

Distance: 6¼ miles/10km	**Type of walk:** *Easy walking; good paths*
Height gain: *360ft/110m*	**Start/Finish:** *Leyburn.*
Walking time: *2½ hours*	*GR112905*

Leyburn, as far east as this book goes, is not dissimilar to Reeth or Grassington. All three founded their prosperity on the mining of lead, all were important market towns, and each continued, in a rather reduced way, when the lead boom collapsed.

In Leyburn, the market place is a delight; a massive

place built to accommodate the folk of the dale, their cattle and wares, their families and conveyances, and much else on market day. Charles II first gave Leyburn its charter, and this was confirmed by James II. Later, the coming of the railway gave an additional boost, but today much of that exciting bustle has gone, and the unkind might say that all Leyburn has today is its shawl. This, far from being the wrap-around comforter that you might suppose, is actually a long walk, a promenade laid out in the 19th century for the well-to-do of Leyburn to exercise themselves along. Romantics like to link Leyburn Shawl with Mary, Queen of Scots who, on managing to escape from her imprisonment at Bolton Castle, reached this high fellside terrace before being recaptured, during the course of which she either lost or threw down her shawl. Blunter minds may point out that 'shawl' is not far from the Norse word 'schalle', which meant a hut or shelter.

Anyway, begin from the centre of town, and leave Leyburn along the Hawes road, following its footpath as far as a wooden gate and stile on the left (just after the dentist's surgery). Go half-left down-field to a gap stile, and then on to cross the old Wensleydale railway line and a small fenced enclosure beyond.

Cross the next field, and when you enter a field with a barn nearby, go left, down-field beside a fence. At the bottom of the field, cross a stile and turn right alongside another fence. From the next stile the path goes slightly left to and through a gate and then across two fields to a gap stile beside a tree stump. From the dead tree go forward beside a wall and cross two fields, then keep on in the

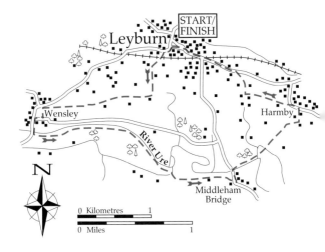

same direction across three more fields to enter Old Glebe Field, a nature reserve.

Continue forward alongside a wall once more and cross a stream by a footbridge. As you leave Old Glebe Field at a stile, turn left along the edge of a small mixed woodland. In the next field, go left down the field edge, turning right at the bottom, alongside a fence, and keep to an obvious path in the next field to reach a large house on the edge of Wensley. Go forward on a green path to a gate and turn left down a surfaced lane. At a T-junction turn right and shortly go up steps into the grounds of Holy Trinity Church.

The church is well worth a visit. It dates from 1240 and is of considerable architectural interest, containing many notable features including some 8th-century Saxon stones, 13th-century windows and 17th-century communion rails and font. John Wesley preached here in 1743.

Wensley, of course, is the village that gives its name to the whole dale, the only village to do so for all the rest are named after their rivers. Even so, to some people the dale is known as Yoredale, after the old name for the river.

Return to follow a grassy path through the graveyard which will lead you out to a squeeze stile giving onto the Hawes road. Turn left and walk down to cross Wensley Bridge, then turn left on a footpath that runs alongside the river.

Keep following the river bank for about one mile (1.6km) and then, as the river makes a pronounced loop, leave it, having crossed an in-flowing stream by a footbridge, and turn right alongside the stream for a few strides. Now bear away from the stream to cross an intermediate track and go forward alongside an old hawthorn hedgerow to meet a stony track. Turn left and follow the track out to meet the A6108, and turn left to cross Middleham Bridge.

On the other side of the bridge, leave the road, on the right, through a metal gate and go forward across the ensuing pasture to a gate and stile. Keep on in the same direction in the next field to cross a bridge, after which bear left to a stony track, signposted to Harmby. Go up the track to a gate, and bear right alongside a fence to a stile in a corner.

Go half-left up the next field and, when it comes into view, head across to a white post marking the location of a gap stile. Through the stile turn right on a surfaced track and, a few strides later, cross a cattle grid and strike obliquely left across the next field to rejoin the surfaced track at a gate and another cattle grid. Through the gate turn left and at a T-junction near the chapel on the edge of Harmby, go left again and walk up the lane for 80yds/m and turn left on a signposted footpath along a surfaced lane.

Two squeeze stiles give access to Manor Farm hay meadow, beyond which keep on across two large open pastures to a bridge spanning a wooded stream. After one more, narrow field, turn right on a stony track. Walk up the track for about 120yds/m and then leave it by going over a stile on the left and across one last field to meet the A684. Turn left along the road and walk into Leyburn.

NIDDERDALE

Most people who venture into Nidderdale these days find the reservoirs – Gouthwaite, Scar House and Angram – a feature that adds immeasurably to the dale rather than detracts from it. Yet, ironically, it was the presence of the reservoirs, and the claim that they despoiled the natural environment, that resulted in Nidderdale being excluded from the Yorkshire Dales National Park when it was designated in 1954.

Notwithstanding such bureaucratic thinking, Roly Smith, Chairman of the Outdoor Writers' Guild, in his book *On Foot in the Yorkshire Dales* asserts, rightly in my view, that Nidderdale is 'the Yorkshire Dales in microcosm', possessing all the qualities and features that have made the Dales famous – 'wild, open moorland; dramatic limestone gorges, caves and pot-holes; weirdly sculpted rocks, and ancient, flower-decked stone villages'.

Forty years later, the dale was made an Area of Outstanding Natural Beauty, a classification that in terms of landscape protection gets as close as is otherwise possible to the standards and criteria that apply in national parks. A sop? Perhaps. Or maybe some latter-day bureaucrat has had greater perception than his predecessors, and, in a modest way, tried to acknowledge that Nidderdale is every bit as deserving of special attention as anywhere else in the Dales.

In *The Yorkshire Pennines of the North-West*, W. Riley writes that Nidderdale is 'the modest maiden of the Pennine Dales, and an altogether delightful region for those who love Nature in her softer moods'. Its eponymous river rises on the tumescent dome of Great Whernside: 'Rising', as Alfred Brown puts it in *Striding through Yorkshire*, 'among the green slopes with a modesty as rare as it is virginal, she slips chastely through the meadows and ends her mortal career as placidly as any nun by the shadow of the old Nunnery at Nun Monkton'. You may be forgiven for thinking that this was written long before the reservoirs appeared, but in fact, it was only fifty years ago, two years after the last of the reservoirs was commissioned.

On its comparatively brief course to join the Ouse, the Nidd gathers a multitude of tributary hill streams before reaching Angram and Scar House reservoirs. Not all the river is impounded by the reservoirs, for below the dam wall of Scar House it continues to flow delightfully until, at Manchester Hole or Goyden Pot (depending on the flow), it disappears underground through a labyrinth of subterranean watercourses not to emerge for two miles (3km) until beyond the village of Lofthouse.

Even then, the water-masters have not done with it for before long it flows into Gouthwaite Reservoir, a compensation reservoir, which, as Harry Scott describes in *Portrait of Yorkshire*, 'has something of the beauty of a Scottish loch'. Of course, it is often the case that wherever reservoirs are built, something disappears in consequence. Here it was Gouthwaite Hall, one of the homes of the Yorke family, who were dominant in the dale from Elizabethan times.

Below the reservoirs and Lofthouse, the Nidd becomes truly a river once more and flows peacefully onwards towards the old market town of Pateley Bridge, which is the key that gives access to the walks in this section of the book, save for the last.

Pateley has a long history. The first settlement was on the hillside above the river, over which there has been a ford and bridge crossing since these early times. The network of tracks and roads that radiate from the town tell of its importance on a number of cross country routes, but notably that linking Fountains Abbey and Bolton Priory. The Archbishops of York, then lords of the manor, granted early fair and market charters, something the townspeople celebrated with a feast in September known as the 'Pateley Rant'.

But there are, however, some attractive villages up-river before you reach the streets of Pateley. Ramsgill, beyond Gouthwaite Reservoir, is a delightful place, where the abbot of Byland Abbey had a chapel, of which only a gable now remains. It is very much a showpiece village with well-flowered gardens fronting attractive cottages around a traditional village green. The Yorke Arms hotel maintains the link with the dale family of that name, and used to be one of the shooting lodges. Nearby Bouthwaite was formerly a grange of Fountains Abbey.

Further on, you reach Lofthouse and Middlesmoor. Both enjoy splendid positions in the dale: the one sitting beside the course of the river, the other perched against the elements on its hill end, with its churchyard providing an unsurpassed view of the dale northwards. Lofthouse occupies a site developed originally by Norse settlers, and, as Jessica Lofthouse (a Lancastrian in spite of the traditional Yorkshire name) describes in *Countrygoer in the Dales*, a village that 'seems more ready to wander away on fell tracks into the cloudy sky rather than down into the dale'. Long-established farms and comely cottages dot the winding street, and are especially attractive in late evening sunlight.

Middlesmoor, set above the dale, it is said 'catches all the sun that's going, and all the four winds of heaven too'. Riley was rather heavy-handed when it came to Middlesmoor, describing it as a 'storm-nipped village...[with] not an atom of beauty about it'. It is, he said, 'as grim a village as any in England'. Not a pretty picture, but, assuming his description was a fair one (and I've no reason to suppose otherwise), one that is no longer true (my opinion, this time). Perhaps the village has mellowed with age, or responded to whatever it is that makes a place attractive both to those who live there and those who visit. Certainly, it does not occupy the most sheltered spot in the dale, but it can no longer be described as grim.

Though now barely in evidence, the dale did once have its own railway. A line from Harrogate to Pateley Bridge was opened in 1862, but closed just over a hundred years later, in 1964. Beyond Pateley Bridge a line continued for another thirteen miles into upper Nidderdale. The Nidd Valley Light Railway was unique in being the only passenger-carrying railway operated by a local authority, Bradford County Borough Council. It was Bradford, of course, that was responsible for building the reservoirs, and the railway was needed to carry building materials. Originally intended to be a narrow gauge line, it was eventually built as standard gauge to avoid having to transfer goods and materials at Pateley Bridge. The line was opened in September 1907, and a public section ran as far as Lofthouse, calling at Wath and Ramsgill. The railway ceased to operate once Scar House Reservoir was completed in 1936, though the passenger service had ended in 1929.

But Nidderdale is not all reservoirs. It is a wild and beautiful landscape of heather and trees, of grouse moors and contrasting green pastures, of potholes, caverns and steep-sided scars. And here, too, are a couple more 'Wonders of the Dales' – the fantastic landscape of weathered gritstone pinnacles at Brimham Rocks and the fascinating limestone gorge at How Stean through which How Stean Beck cascades on its way to join the River Nidd.

And if this is not enough, then content yourself with the knowledge that in this book I have concentrated only on that part of Nidderdale that reaches beyond Brimham Rocks and Pateley Bridge to Nidd Head; there is much more to this area of outstanding natural beauty than I have encompassed here.

30 Scar House Reservoir

Although this walk around one of the upper Nidderdale reservoirs is quite short, it does combine easily with Walk 31 to give a longer circuit. The reservoirs were built early in the 20th century by Bradford Corporation, and their dam walls are quite spectacular constructions of considerable architectural merit. The road up to the reservoirs is a private one beyond the village of Lofthouse, and there is a nominal toll payable at the entrance: the simple delight of travelling up this often neglected dale makes it worthwhile.

Distance: 4¼ miles/7km   *level walk*
Height gain: *Nominal*   **Start/Finish:** *Reservoir*
Walking time: *2 hours*   *car park. GR069766*
Type of walk: *Easy,*

The route description is the simplest possible: simple walk round the reservoir. From the car park, which has picnic tables nearby and toilets, a surfaced road leads westward and along the southern shore towards the uppermost reservoir, Angram, with the imposing bulk of Great Whernside as a backdrop.

Over the years, reservoirs generally have been guilty of

destroying beautiful tracts of countryside, and they have effected, here in the Dales, radical changes to the scenery. Thankfully, those that occupy Nidderdale are something of an exception, and actually complement the landscape. Gouthwaite, lower down the valley, is popular with birdwatchers, while the upper reservoirs – Angram was completed in 1914 and Scar House in 1936 – do much, in their way, to enhance what W. Riley (in 'The Yorkshire Pennines of the North-West') describes as '...this hush of green solitudes, these wooded glens stealing quietly down the fellsides to the river's bank...' It is quite a pleasure to be in their midst.*

The on-going road eventually reaches Angram Reservoir at a rest house, a small shelter provided by the water company.

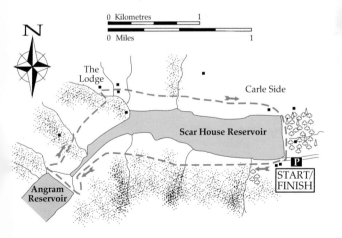

Angram is the smaller of the two reservoirs, and its making drowned a small farmstead, the uppermost in the dale, which stood on a site occupied by a grange belonging to Byland Abbey.

Cross the reservoir dam, and go through a gate onto a path striking right across tumbled down walls to more gates before reaching the end of a green lane, and swinging up to the ruins of the Lodge, a former hunting lodge and farm.

The lane that runs to the Lodge, and continues beyond, is Carle Fell Road, an ancient market road by which cattle drovers, packhorse men, traders and customers would travel to markets and fairs at Masham.

Carle Fell Road now takes you back towards the dam of Scar House Reservoir.

Just before descending to the dam, a second track branches left (signposted: Nidderdale Way). If you want to combine this walk with Walk 31, this is where you would turn off. Of course, you can always return to the car for refreshments, and then do the second walk.

Cross the dam and turn left to return to your starting point.

31 Upper Nidderdale

*No one seems certain these days about why it was that
Nidderdale, as beautiful a Dales landscape as any, was
excluded from the boundaries of the Yorkshire Dales
National Park. You have only to follow this walk across
the hillsides just below the dam of Scar House Reservoir
to see for yourself what an attractive valley this is. At
least it was accorded some status when it was designated
an Area of Outstanding Natural Beauty in 1994: in
many ways that says it all – an area of outstanding
natural beauty.*

Distance: *6¹/₂ miles/
10.5km*
Height gain: *820ft/250m*
Walking time: *3-4 hours*
Type of walk: *Moderate*

*walking on paths and
tracks*
Start/Finish: *Scar House
car park. GR069766*

*Upper Nidderdale provides some excellent walking that
is both rewarding and at times demanding. Poor weather
makes the distances seem much greater than they are,
but on a fine day many visitors will experience a marked
reluctance to leave. The scenery is as good as anything
you get in the Dales, and north of Lofthouse is quite
outstanding. Beyond the upper reservoirs rises the
sprawling mound of Great Whernside, while its lesser
companion, Little Whernside, perches boggily above
Angram Reservoir.*

Start from the car park near the dam of Scar House Reservoir and go left to cross the dam. On the other side climb left on a stony track for about 100yds/m and then branch right on the Nidderdale Way, which here runs across the slopes of Carle Fell. The track rises gradually onto the moor and passes a stand of larch trees. A short way further on it dips to cross a stream in a gully, rising on the other side back onto the moor edge. Follow the on-going track until you can leave it, on the right, pursuing a descending line of white-topped marker posts, and heading to and through a gate. Beyond the gate, follow a broad green track descending right and then doubling back.

Keep following the track down through two more gates, and then go left as the track runs alongside a wall towards New Houses Edge Farm. When the track forks, about a quarter of a mile before the farm, branch left and keep going past the farm.

About 300yds/m before a plantation, the track forks once more. Keep right this time, heading towards the plantation, and shortly zigzag down past a farm and then follow the on-going track to reach Thwaite House Farm. Go past the farm and descend, right, zigzagging down to cross a streambed at the rear of Limley Farm.

Go forward to turn right around a large barn and follow a track through the farm buildings. As you pass the last stone building on the left, turn right and go in front of a farmhouse to a gate, and onto a path running alongside the River Nidd, which is often a dry riverbed – the river having disappeared underground.

Keep on alongside the river, ignoring any stiles across fences on either side, until you can cross the river by a footbridge. Over the bridge turn left and walk towards a gate a short distance away. Beyond the gate follow a riverside path alongside a fence, and continue to a bridge just past New Houses Farm.

Ignore the bridge, and keep forward on a stony vehicle track beside the river. Never far from the river, the path keeps on as far as Low Woodale Farm. Go forward between the farm buildings and turn left to go over a bridge. Follow the rising access track out to meet the main valley road above. There turn right and walk back to the car park at Scar House.

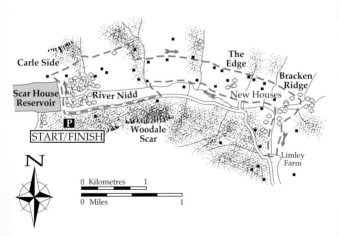

32 How Stean Gorge

The gorge at How Stean is a deep, limestone ravine through which How Stean Beck plunges on its way to join the River Nidd below the village of Lofthouse. This walk, however, goes a little further and reaches to the village of Middlesmoor, where, from its hill-top churchyard, there is a splendid view up the dale. After Middlesmoor, we head into that view, before returning on the opposite side of the Nidd.

Distance: 4¼ miles/7km	uphill, then moderate
Height gain:	*walking*
625ft/190m	**Start/Finish:** *Lofthouse.*
Walking time: *2-3 hours*	*GR101735*
Type of walk: *Brief*	

Opposite the post office in Lofthouse, a track runs between cottages and soon leads to a footbridge over the River Nidd. Once over the river, cross to the Scar House road and a gate. Continue between a barn and a playing field to another gate in a wall corner, beyond which you meet the Middlesmoor road. Turn right for a few strides, then branch left on the road for Stean.

Having crossed How Stean Beck, follow the road as it turns right to go past the entrance to How Stean Gorge.

There is a fee to be paid for visiting the gorge, and this natural feature is not to be missed. The whole area of the gorge, however, is fascinating, and time should be added to allow for exploration. How Stean Tunnel is especially interesting, while Tom Taylor's Chamber, said to be named after a local freebooter, is a massive cave that extends into the field behind the cafe. The cave can be explored with the aid of a torch.

You can resume the walk by either of two ways. One involves returning to the main road and turning right to walk as far as a stile at a footpath (signposted to Middlesmoor); the other crosses the bridge to the car park field, and then heads for a gate in the top left corner. From there go past a barn, then bear left across fields to meet the Middlesmoor path above.

The path soon crosses How Stean Beck, with another impromptu view of the gorge, and goes up steps to a gate. Beyond the gate, head for a wall gap on the right, and then turn left. The Nidderdale Way now takes you across fields to meet the lane into Middlesmoor.

Middlesmoor is a delightful place, perched high above the dale, at the end of a ridge, similar to Reeth, but with much more elevation. The village church, St Chad's – which contains a 7th-century Saxon cross – and churchyard are particular gems.

Walk up towards the village. Go along the road, pass the pub and the post office, and just after the last building on the right, turn right onto a track, but go immediately left through a gate to pursue a grassy path past a car park. Cross a stile and go forward with a wall on your left to another stile and the western edge of a narrow plantation. Pass through a gap and tend right in the next field to another stile, and from it keep ahead.

Keep on in the same direction across more fields and heading for a track that runs to Northside Head Farm. Turn right along the track and continue beyond the farm, initially still on a track, and then, further on, alongside a wall on your right, to reach a gate at the edge of How Gill Plantation. Here turn right, go through another gate, and begin descending. Move left to cross a stream, and then head for a fence/wall corner.

Cross a stile, and head for the bottom left-hand corner of the ensuing pasture. Climb some stone steps, then go ahead to a stile, and beyond that head obliquely across the next pasture to another stile. After that, and a fence, you soon reach the Scar House road once more.

Cross the road and the field opposite to reach Limley Farm. As you reach the farm buildings turn right onto its access track, soon leaving it, on the left, as it turns up to the road. More of the Nidderdale Way now follows as it accompanies the Nidd all the way back to Lofthouse.

Not long after leaving the farm, the route crosses the course of the Nidd, which at certain times of year disappears underground and so doesn't always have water in it. Across the river, you pick up a track known as Thrope Lane. With excellent views of the dale from its slightly elevated course, this leads you to a road directly into Lofthouse.

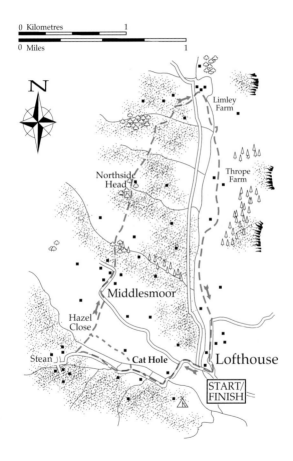

33 Wath

This short walk from Pateley Bridge is laden with interest, and illustrates the range of man's influence in the dale far better, perhaps, than can be seen from any other spot. If the delightful buildings of Pateley Bridge, a fine old market town, are not enough, then along the hillsides above you encounter evidence of forestry and quarrying. Here, too, is a light railway used in the construction of the up-dale reservoirs, and with the benefit of elevation you can see the first of those reservoirs, Gouthwaite, and look further to the remains of the lead mining industry that flourished in the area centuries ago. The walk concludes along the banks of the Nidd.

Distance: *4 miles/6km* *walking*
Height gain: *555ft/170m* **Start/Finish:** *Pateley*
Walking time: *2-3 hours* *Bridge car park.*
Type of walk: *Easy* *GR157656*

Begin from the car park near the river bridge, and turn right up High Street. At the top, turn left into Church Street and go past St Cuthbert's church and along Wath Road.

After the last house on the left, the road crosses a bridge, and a stile gives access to a grassy incline, which leads steeply to the extensive site of the Scot Gate Ash Quarry above.

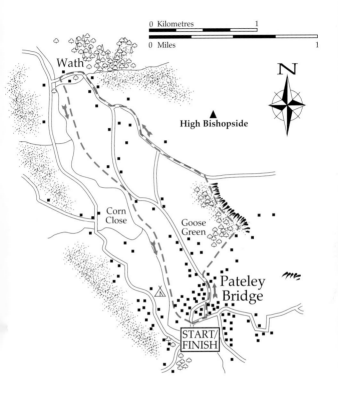

The quarry was an important source of employment, and produced a form of gritstone known as 'delphstone', a particularly resilient rock that went into many major buildings – the National Gallery and Victoria Station in London, for example – for use as flagstones and steps in particular. In the late 19th century, the stone was sent down the incline you

163

have just ascended directly to the railway yard at Pateley Bridge.

As you face the terminal of the tramway, head for a track bearing left alongside a fence and wall. The ensuing path guides you across the edge of the quarry to a gate, and from there cross a field to reach a narrow lane, Wath Lane.

Now turn left and follow the lane towards the hamlet of Wath. At a junction go forward to another junction at Pie Gill Green, and there turn right to enter Wath.

As you walk along Wath Lane so you are treated to a superb panorama. Up-dale lies Gouthwaite Reservoir, another touch of man's hand, while in the opposite direction the natural horizon is despoiled by the intrusive 'golf balls' on Menwith Hill. Across the dale you can see into the dale of Ashfold Side Beck, where the old Merryfield lead mines are found.

Follow the road through Wath, passing the Sportsmans Arms, and shortly you reach Wath Bridge over the Nidd.

The bridge is clearly a packhorse bridge, and this superseded a ford at this spot. This one is thought to have been built by the monks of Byland Abbey, who were allowed to use a route from Heathfield across the Fountains estates. It is almost certain that the monasteries housed the first bridge builders in many of the dales.

Don't cross the river bridge, but opt for a smaller,

less imposing footbridge on the left. Now walk onward to reach the course of the Nidd Valley Light Railway, built by Bradford Corporation, and used during the construction of the reservoirs, though it did run a passenger service for about twenty years until the 1930s.

The course of the old railway line is followed for some distance, as it heads back to Pateley Bridge. After a stile you leave the railway for the riverside, being guided by its delightful, tree-lined banks back towards Pateley Bridge. On the outskirts of the town, the path is diverted away from the river to pass between buildings and onto a lane that takes you back to the start.

34 Merryfield Mines

The Merryfield Mines lie along a tributary dale, west of Pateley Bridge, biting into the flanks of Heathfield and Hardcastle moors. The walk is suitable for all seasons, but involves crossing a shallow ford that sometimes isn't shallow: a small hand towel might on this occasion be useful additions to the rucksack. The moors are a delight, dotted as they are with isolated farms, and home to a variety of birds, including meadow pipit, skylark, snipe, curlew and woodcock.

Distance: *5½ miles/9km*	*walking on good tracks*
Height gain: *590ft/*	*and field paths*
180m	**Start/Finish:** *Pateley*
Walking time: *3 hours*	*Bridge. GR157656*
Type of walk: *Easy*	

Start from the car park at the bottom of High Street, adjoining Pateley Bridge. Cross the bridge and head towards the Royal Oak pub and turn right just before it. Immediately before reaching the Old (Metcalfe's) Brewery, turn left between cottages onto a rising lane, soon going forward along a grassy track to a gate, and then climbing steadily into an open pasture. Keep to its left-hand edge and climb to a gate in a wall corner at the top of the field.

Go through the gate and forward with a wall on

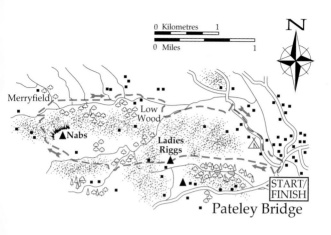

your left-hand side as you pass Eagle Hall. The wall eventually gives way to a hedgerow and fence, and leads up to a through stile. After this turn right, and in a few strides join a surfaced lane, part of the Nidderdale Way, which will feature in much of the walk to come.

The view improves all the time, but as you reach the high point in the lane, an especially pleasant scene opens up ahead, of rolling, sparsely wooded hillsides studded with isolated farms.

As you approach Hill End Farm the surfacing ends, but the lane, which turns first right and then left, continues as a farm access that takes you on through delightful scenery. The track crosses Brandstone Beck at Brandstone Dub Bridge, and beyond climbs left on a stony track.

At the remains of the Merryfield mines, a once-important source of lead ore, the track forks. Here branch right (though if you want to explore the area it doesn't matter which way you go), descending on a grassy track to meet a stony track lower down, just as Ashfold Side Beck comes into view. As it does so, on the opposite side, you can see a gate; this is your objective, and to reach it the beck has to be forded. Normally this is easily accomplished at a concrete ford just below the gate.

If you cannot cross, the only lawful option, not an altogether unpalatable one, is to retrace your steps.

On the other side, climb a little higher, diagonally right, to a broad track that once served the mines.

Head off down the track, shortly turning away from the main beck to cross Rowantree Gill before resuming your original course.

When you reach a caravan site, the first of a number that now flank the route, the on-going track is surfaced once more. Keep on until you meet the entrance to Low Wood Caravan Site on the right (small Nidderdale Way signpost). Go through a gate and forward to cross the beck, then bear right beyond a second gate on a rising track that soon becomes a delightful green lane between walls. This leads down to a footbridge at Mosscarr Bottom. Immediately after the footbridge, turn left through a red metal gate at the side of a cottage. Go forward on a gravel track to pass in front of the cottage, and onward through another gate. Beyond, a vehicle track leads across farmland to Mosscarr Farm.

Cross a cattle grid near the farm, and then bear left, continuing along an access track, which you now follow until it meets a road. Turn right, and follow the road towards Pateley Bridge, taking particular care along those stretches that do not have a footpath.

On the edge of Pateley Bridge, just after a caravan site on your left, go through a gap in a low wall on the left, and follow a paved path to the embankment of the River Nidd, and there turn right along a surfaced pathway along the edge of playing fields. The path returns you directly to Pateley Bridge.

35 Brimham Rocks

Such is the fascination of the weird gritstone monoliths at Brimham Moor that many visitors content themselves with wandering the network of pathways in a kind of bewildered exploration, as if unable to believe that the agents of erosion alone could produce such a bizarre spectacle. In fact, the early visitors to Brimham credited the Druids with having a hand in the design, as many of the names given to the outcrops confirm – Druid's Writing Desk, Druid's Cave, and so on. But the reality is that all the rock formations are the work of Mother Nature, painstaking work with rain, wind and frost as assistants.

Distance: *6 miles/10km*
Height gain: *575ft/175m*
Walking time: *3-4 hours*
Type of walk: *Easy*

walking on good paths
Start/Finish: *Brimham Rocks NT car park.*
GR208646

From the National Trust car park you can either follow a broad track that leads directly to Brimham House or, if preferred, immediately wander off up a path to the left of it, instantly meeting up with the rock formations. Before long Brimham House comes into view, to which you should head whenever your exploration of the Rocks is complete.

Lord Grantley built Brimham House in the late 18th century for his gamekeeper, and its size and grandeur gives you some idea how important the job was at the time. There is a small refreshment kiosk nearby, and toilets, while the house itself is a shop and information point.

Immediately to the side (left) of Brimham House you encounter 'The Dancing Bear', a towering formation that does indeed look like a dancing bear. By following the path round, with the occasional diversion to take in the far-reaching panorama, you soon reach another, almost unbelievable formation, the 'Idol', or 'Druid's Idol', a massive rock balanced on a tiny pedestal.

Beyond this, the path takes you out of the light woodland cover that surrounds the Rocks. Here the path turns back to the right, and here you should leave it for a narrow path striking northward and dropping to meet a wider path. Turn left along it, and return to woodland, until, on the far side, you can turn right on a path leading across fields to North Pasture Farm.

Go through the farm on a track that eventually takes you out to the B6265. Turn left towards the village of Fell Beck and the Half Moon Inn. Beyond the pub, climb up the road and then turn left at the first farm buildings at Knoll Top. Go through a gate and turn right to a stile before descending beside a wall to another stile, and gate, beyond. Now go through trees soon to reach a stream, also called Fell Beck.

Follow a streamside path and pass a small lake and keep on until you reach a walled track. Here, turn to cross a footbridge on the left, and then continue on a path that steadily climbs away from the beck and goes on to pass the buildings at Low Wood Farm. Now continue southward, gradually descending to the beck once more, and recrossing it by another footbridge.

Continue following the stream until you reach the hamlet of Smelthouses, its name a reminder, the only reminder, of the lead mining industry that once flourished here from as early as the 14th century. Turn left at the road and cross Fell Beck Bridge, and then turn right, descending to reach the main dale road at Low Laithes. Turn left.

Opposite the pub turn onto a bridleway that climbs to the road above, at Wise Ing (Wysing). Turn left at the road and soon turn right on a surfaced track to Low Wood House. Go through a gate on the right onto a green lane, formerly used by the monks of Fountains Abbey. This, mainly walled but later running alongside a fence, will lead you through High Wood and a few gates eventually to meet a road. Turn left for about 300yds/m, then branch left to return to the Brimham Rocks car park.

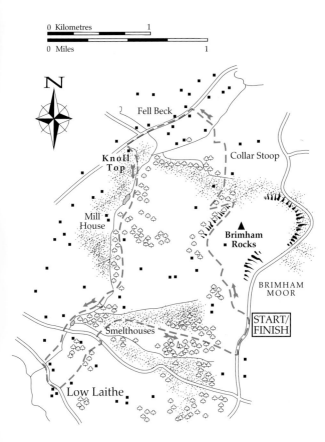

0 Kilometres 1

0 Miles 1

N

Fell Beck

Knoll Top

Collar Stoop

Mill House

Brimham Rocks

Low Laithe

Smelthouses

BRIMHAM MOOR

START/ FINISH

Other Dalesman titles for walkers

Walking and Trail Guides
Lake District Western Fells Paddy Dillon £4.99
Lake District Eastern Fells Paddy Dillon £4.99
Yorkshire Dales South & West Terry Marsh £4.99

Walks Around Series: Yorkshire
Grassington Richard Musgrave £1.99
Hawes Richard Musgrave £1.99
Helmsley Nick Channer £1.99
Kirkbymoorside Nick Channer £1.99
Pickering Nick Channer £1.99
Richmond Richard Musgrave £1.99
Settle & Malham Richard Musgrave £1.99
Whitby Nick Channer £1.99

Walks Around Series: Lake District
Ambleside Tom Bowker £1.99
Coniston & Hawkshead Mary Welsh £1.99
Keswick Dawn Gibson £1.99
Windermere Robert Gambles £1.99

Pub Walks Series
Lancashire Terry Marsh £5.99
Lake District Terry Marsh £5.99
Peak District John Morrison £5.99
North York Moors & Coast Richard Musgrave £5.99

Tea Shop Walks Series
Lake District Mary Welsh £5.99
Yorkshire Dales Richard Musgrave £5.99
North York Moors & Coast Mark Reid £5.99